MOUNTAIN GIANTS OF THE ADIRONDACKS

JASON LOREFICE

BEYOND THE FRAY

Publishing

Published by Beyond The Fray Publishing

ISBN 13: 978-1-954528-71-0
Cover design: Dauntless Cover Design

Beyond The Fray Publishing, a division of Beyond The Fray, LLC, San Diego, CA
www.beyondthefraypublishing.com

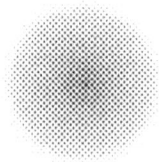

BEYOND THE FRAY

Publishing

SPECIAL THANKS TO
Lind Godfrey
Emily of the Forest Fleur
Dogmancryptids
North American Dogman Project
Frank Siecienski
Steve Lynch

CONTENTS

INTRODUCTION

Bigfoot, Sasquatch, Yeti, Wildman, Mountain Giants, Skunk Ape, Mountain Devil, Skookum, Grassman, Yowie. These unknown hairy hominids go by many names. Yet thousands of people in North America and around the globe have reported seeing or encountering tall, hair-covered creatures resembling half human and half primate. Researchers have investigated countless cases and collected hair samples, analyzed photos and videos along with audio recordings of what is believed to be them screaming in the night. But what do we really know about these hairy hominids and other mysterious cryptids running around in our woods? We know a lot. We don't have a body, but we do have DNA to tell their story.

As researchers, we gather as much information as best we can and build a case with sometimes very little to go on. As we venture into the woods or swamps in search of these elusive hominids, it's important to maintain ethical integrity of all living beings. On Amazon you will find over a hundred books devoted to the subject of Bigfoot. And because there is so much written on the topic, those of us who write about it have examined the evidence and have formed our own personal opinions on the origins of their habitat. Over the years movies and television have embraced the phenomenon of Bigfoot and its ability to promote revenue, sell videos, books, and movies all for the motive to grow profits. And with the growing popularity of Sasquatch, it has since fueled the fire to invest in researching the science of these elusive beings. The 1970s era has given us the weekly documentary show *In Search Of*, hosted by Leonard Nimoy, exploring the strange, the mysterious and the unknown, which touched on the topic of Sasquatch in a similar fashion.

Those of us who volunteer our time and efforts to validate these creatures and ultimately ensure their protection work timelessly to achieve this goal. The countless hours we spend in the woods, the travel time we invest on the road, witness interviewing and evidence analyzing, have brought results, but there is more out there to discover. When we tell people that we hunt for Sasquatch, they look at us rather strangely, or possibly are taken aback by our interest. Every piece of evidence we gather is one more piece of the puzzle in order to create a picture we can present to the scientific community to prove our case.

A new survey from the Travel Channel and Bigfoot Field Researchers Organization shows New York has some of the highest reported Bigfoot sightings. The report says New York finished fifth in the United States behind Washington, California, Pennsylvania and Michigan in sightings of the mythical creature. According to the Bigfoot Field Researchers Organization's website, there have been only two reported sightings in Monroe County, with the last in 2005. The Travel Channel says Whitehall, NY, which is near the Vermont border, is considered the "Bigfoot capital of the East Coast."

In 2020, New Yorkers reported 113 Bigfoot sightings, according to Microsoft News. For north country residents, Bigfoot is believed to be residing in their backyards. While discussions about Bigfoot can seem rather recent in our United States history, Native Americans have talked about Sasquatch for hundreds of years. Often considered a West Coast phenomenon, sightings have also appeared all over the Adirondacks, from Saranac Lake in the north to a famous sighting in Whitehall, to Lake George and in the southern foothills. If this is indeed a myth, it is a remarkably durable one.

THE ADIRONDACKS

The Adirondack Mountains are formed in northeastern Upstate New York, with boundaries that correspond roughly to those of Adirondack Park. They cover about five thousand square miles. The mountains form a roughly circular dome, about 160 miles in diameter and about 1 mile high. The current relief owes much to glaciation. There are more than two hundred lakes around the mountains, including Lake George, Lake Placid, and Lake Tear of the Clouds, which is the source of the Hudson River. The Adirondack region is also home to hundreds of mountain summits, with some reaching heights of five thousand feet or more.

The Adirondacks were originally claimed by two Indian nations, the Iroquois and the Algonquins. Neither group ever settled in the region, but the two nations fought over the Lake George-Lake Champlain water route through the Adirondacks. This route was the easiest one through the Adirondacks and was therefore a valuable resource. Dating back to the 1700s, the Adirondacks were a popular destination, with Lake George and Lake Champlain providing ideal conditions for settlements and later for military posts.

Opportunities abound to see examples of the evolution of Adirondack architecture, of both the real McCoy and reproduction varieties. The last 250 years in the Adirondacks have produced a bounty of historic intrigue. Like the infinite hikes within the park, the history here is accessible - walk the trails, ride the trains, and visit the places written about in textbooks and novels alike.

As all citizens in any country know, government is not your friend. It's also no secret they treat the people like children by keeping them in the dark when it comes to their own dirty secrets. We've known that various levels of government have acknowledged that these creatures exist, and some states have enacted legislation in protecting them from being hunted or killed by us humans. However, government will avoid putting themselves in any awkward situations when they can't defend their positions. And government employees don't want to create embarrassment for the fear of any backlash. The idea that Bigfoot exists in our areas is always the number one issue that we are searching for and attempting to document.

Hair samples from alleged Sasquatches analyzed by FBI laboratories resulted in the conclusion that no such hair exists on any human or known animal in our databanks of species identification. Information from eyewitness reports, including tracks, hair samples and other physical evidence, supports the fact that we are dealing with large hairy hominids living among us in our wild forests and national parks. The height of these hominids can vary between seven to ten feet, while weighing an excess of six hundred to nine hundred pounds or more. Over the years numerous plaster casts have been made of trackways showing a foot length between fourteen to twenty inches in length. Physical descriptions vary in color, height, and facial features but most commonly are covered with hair with the exceptions of the face and hands.

According to findings, Some Bigfoot researchers believe it is a giant, anthropoid, humanlike creature, large, very hairy, and very smelly. This could explain the report of a highly pungent, neglected-human smell in a wilderness area. Regardless of your belief, people have been reporting their encounters with these hominids long before there was a mass reporting of this phenomenon and long before the term "Bigfoot" was phrased. Over the years researchers have collected hundreds of eyewitness accounts of encounters in the Adirondacks of a large hairy creature known as "Bigfoot." Some of them are seemingly simple, like the reports of rocks being thrown at people.

Investigations into the subject are very fragmented, with researchers and organizations reluctant to share findings and evidence with others. Since 2001, there have been well over two thousand Bigfoot sightings on file in North America. However, the United States Justice Department states that on average 10% of all rape cases are ever reported. Why aren't 100% of them reported? The answer is public humiliation, fear of embarrassment, threats and intimidation, anxiety and emotional trauma. If society as a whole treated witnesses differently on sensitive issues, people would feel more confident coming forward. Therefore, if two thousand are on file, we can estimate at least twenty thousand plus sightings have actually been witnessed and not reported.

MIGRATION

With a creature such as Bigfoot, it seems unlikely that that they would remain in any one area for very long. It's more likely they would follow food such as deer and edible plants as they migrate or were in season. Many animals do this so as not to denude any one location and for their own survival. To understand Bigfoot migration patterns and where to search, it's important to understand geographic distribution and environmental surroundings. It's also just as important to understand its food source, such as deer, and its competitors for its food. And once you have an understanding of how these hominids migrate, access their food, where their food is located, and the amount of food available, then you will have a better understanding of the creature itself.

Sightings of these hominids have been reported in almost all fifty states, with California, Washington, Oregon and Texas having the highest reports of sightings. Learning about the practical application of math and statistics will lend a better understanding about their behavior, hot-spot areas, migration, travel routes and food sources. Some animals, like whitetail deer, migrate to a certain degree in wilderness areas, while other whitetails, such as those in the rural non-wilderness areas of eastern North America and other rural areas, will stay in the same small tract of land for their entire lifespans and never migrate as long as there's enough food to sustain them. Since deer and elk and other grazing animals are believed to be a favorite food source for Bigfoot, this may explain at least some of the beliefs that they might possibly migrate in some areas. They're following the food source.

It's become apparent that a large number of Bigfoot reports in New York were centered in the northern part of the state located in the northern Adirondacks. A more controversial hypothesis is the alleged correlation between bears and Bigfoot. Many Bigfoot researchers have stated that Bigfoot is located in areas where there are bears. The more bears, the more Bigfoot. To rationalize this theory into better understanding, the more bears, the more food sources, the more food sources would mean more Bigfoot. It's evident that these two species share the same dietary practice here in the

East Coast. According to the United States Forest Services, there are approximately six hundred thousand black bears in the United States. These bears can range from two hundred to seven hundred pounds and can live up to thirty years if not hunted. The Forestry Services estimates there are approximately five thousand black bears in Vermont and over eighteen thousand in the upstate area of the Adirondacks. The question that science needs to ask is, "Is there a correlation between the number of bears in a specific area and the number of Bigfoot?"

It should be obvious at this point that these large hominids in both the western part of the United States and the East Coast both prefer areas that have large annual rainfall in addition to heavily forested areas. And Upstate New York provides just the place for them. The idea of a creature such as Bigfoot can seem rather recent in our United States history, but Native Americans have talked about Sasquatch for hundreds of years.

Often considered a West Coast phenomenon, sightings have also appeared all over the Adirondacks, from Lake George to Saranac Lake in the north to a famous sighting in Whitehall, in the southern foothills. There are several criteria that can be used to measure which county has the highest volume of Bigfoot activity. The most obvious being the number of eyewitness reports. In a country primarily composed of land mass and forest, the number of sightings may not be an accurate volume of Bigfoot activity compared to a relatively small county.

The odds of one having an encounter with a Sasquatch can rely on a number of different variables. However, after interviewing many eyewitnesses native to the area, I have notice approximately eight out of ten sightings witness the creature crossing the road during the late night hours, with the vast majority of these sightings taking place between the hours of 7 p.m. to 7 a.m., and over 90% of those encounters take place near bodies of water. But we do have to reconcile that the vast majority of people are not outside during the hours of 12 a.m. to 4 a.m.; therefore a Bigfoot report could not be made. Roadside encounters appear to dominate the typical campers and hunters scenario that one would expect when spending ample time in the mountains. The behavior and activity that is likely attributed to Bigfoot may include rock throwing, screaming, foul odors, glowing red eyes, footprints, tree knocks, humanlike vocalizations, and the sense of being followed while in the woods.

As early humans we survived by hunting in groups such as tribal units. By working as a team, we were able to take down large prey to feed and support the members of our tribe. With Sasquatch creatures, I have found clear indications that they also travel in family units, most likely consisting of a male leader, a female, and one to three young juveniles. It has been my conclusion that the male would have developed strong hunting tactics to ensure the survival of the family.

Living in the deep woods of North America, the primary source of protein would be prey animals such as deer, elk or moose, which are available all year round. An omnivorous lifestyle would also increase their opportunity to obtain proper nutrition. Hunting these animals would require them to be masters of their environment as well as having superior speed and strength to overpower their prey. As humans, we use technology such as rifles, traps, and other hunting accessories. Having the ability to move through the forest without alerting the deer in the area takes some knowledge. A solitary hominid using some stealth could take down a substantial-size animal using upper-body strength or an accurately thrown rock to its head. Passing this ability onto its young would be essential for their survival.

Doing research into my own area of Vermont gave me a

certain perspective on this possibility. For years the only place a Bigfoot would have to hide here are inside patches of woods or forests alongside crop fields, but with our vast green mountains, there are plenty of forested areas for them to travel and go undetected for many years. The humans have sadly taken over everything else here. Some areas that remain are almost too small to call habitats for a creature that could possibly weigh upwards of four hundred to eight hundred pounds and be up to ten feet tall. For years, I didn't think it was possible for them to exist here at all until the evidence changed my mind.

Activity here appears most noticeable in the spring and increases in early fall, and ends or slows down in winter. It has been my speculation that it's about having enough cover to maintain survival, like hide, eat, and mate. At least in my area, they do seem to migrate. Based on my research and logging times and dates and locations, a pattern began to emerge. During the spring, in early May into June, we start to see activity (reports) in the lower elevations of the Adirondacks. During midsummer, reports become less frequent. And into August to late October, activity becomes more frequent again. This is a clear indication of travel routes used during seasonal times of the year. In the spring, I find new stick structures, broken trees, and footprints. However, as the leaves fall in autumn, this activity seems to slow. And when the trees are bare and the landscape is stark, there's no longer any evidence of activity. So I theorize there's no place left for them to hide in those areas at that time of year, so they remain on the go. But in an area such as the Adirondacks, where there are unlimited areas suitable for hiding in winter, I have mentioned the possibility of caves.

ELEVATION

As I first started to investigate reports of Bigfoot in the Adirondacks, I started to look for patterns and common denominators in the groups of sightings. Each time I went out to visit a sighting location, I documented the elevation, and quickly, I saw there was a connection with elevation. Hilltops and mountains collect the most snow because they stay colder longer than the valleys, so more of storms' moisture falls as snow and less as rain. Virgil sits at 1,424 feet above sea level. Erieville is 1,499 feet. In northern New York, the Adirondack region has an average seasonal snowfall in excess of ninety inches, but amounts decrease to sixty to seventy inches in the lowlands of the St. Lawrence Valley and to about sixty inches in the vicinity of Lake Champlain. In the Catskill region, average seasonal snowfall is in excess of fifty inches, with higher snow totals at the mountain base areas than in the villages, and far more than falls in the Hudson Valley. Much of the snow in the Catskills is from nor'easters, which are almost always snow.

This is not to imply that sightings don't take place in other elevations, because they do. However, it would appear that these hominids like moderate climates and the ability to move in and out of different zones as weather changes. The 1,500-to-2,000-foot elevation allows these hominids to drop lower when the weather gets colder, and it also allows them to step up into higher elevations as the seasons get warmer. Deer and elk tend to move into higher elevations and down into the coastal range as winter and summer come and go, and 1,500 to 2,000 feet may be the optimum elevation for Bigfoot activity. It doesn't appear that Bigfoot is affected by snow as much as the other wildlife and regularly travels to here in New England for hunting and gathering, then returns to its nesting ground.

Interviewing witnesses is entirely different than interviewing victims and suspects. The witness usually doesn't have the same invested interest in the outcome of the issue as a victim or suspect. The witness interview can sometimes reveal more information than any interview that takes place. Suspect interviews are much different than the victim or witness interviews. Suspects tend to be more evasive or sometimes even confrontational. Methods of interview will vary with location, background of suspect, and time of the incident. Among the many witnesses I have interviewed (hunters, woodsmen, hikers, campers, fishermen, locals), I have never had a witness mistake a bear for a moose, or a human for a bear, nor will you have a person mistake a motorcycle for a truck. People who are familiar with this environment simply don't make those mistakes. In my years of investigating this phenomenon, I've had many friends and coworkers question me about the validity of the existence of Bigfoot. After all, it's human nature to want to question things such as this. And many of the witnesses I have interviewed were not willing to go on camera for fear of ridicule but are adamant about what they saw.

I have also noticed more documentaries, such as History Channel, *MonsterQuest*, and other independent filmmakers producing episodes on the subject of Bigfoot; there are in turn more eyewitnesses coming forth and sharing their stories and experiences. This is a huge plus for us researchers.

CAVES

In 2015 I met with a friend of mine who had a career in law enforcement with the US Marshals. We were on the subject of fugitive-tracking methods, and the concept of caves was brought up. While New York is home to dozens of known caves, it's highly possible that there are hundreds of other caves that have yet to be discovered. One of the most thought-provoking theories for Bigfoot's overwhelming elusiveness suggests that the creatures spend a great deal of time living in natural caves and caverns, as well as abandoned old mines.

The Almasty is the Russian equivalent of Bigfoot. Not only that, there were reports of strange, large footprints having been discovered in the depths of nearby caves. Scientists found two identical yeti footprints. One of them was left in the rock, and it dates back five thousand years, and the other footprint, which was left not long ago, was found at the bottom of the cave.

Situated on the northern coast of South America, Guyana is a place that, like so many other locales dominated by thick jungles and high mountains, can boast of being the domain of a Bigfoot-style habitat. It is known by the people of Guyana as the "Didi." Interestingly, although the Didi resembles Bigfoot in the sense of it having a humanoid-looking form and being covered in hair, there is one big difference. The creature of Guyana possesses razor-sharp claws, which is a variance of other primates. This has given rise to the theory that the Didi may actually be a creature known as *Megatherium*, a huge sloth that died out thousands of years ago. Or did it? Many witnesses to the Didi have made claims to its eerie humanlike appearance.

Usually cave temperature is figured as the average between the surface high and low. At a lower elevation, the annual high is approximately 68 degrees F, and the winter low is 40 degrees F. The caves would be a great place to escape temperature extremes or to leave offspring behind while the adults hunted.

It should be kept in mind that people exploring caves are part of a close-knit society where information is shared only in the groups. Often in the Bigfoot world, individuals come across something they can't explain and are eager to put a label on it. Caves are good environments for the preservation of artifacts and animal remains that out in the open would be disposed of by nature. Very seldom do I come across deer bones in the woods, and never have I found bear bones in the forests either. But I have found them in caves. Bigfoot might use a cave but not habitually. But their apparent intelligence leads me to believe they might possibly use them during the seasonal winter months.

LOCATION

As I gather reports and eyewitness accounts, I begin to see a pattern that clusters in areas in the Upstate New York region. These areas of interest have seasonal reports during specific times of the year, while other areas have reports in opposing months. The farther north I accumulated sightings data in New York, the more a distinct pattern emerged. As I accumulated the data in the state of New York, I noticed a pattern of sightings in the northeastern part of the state. I took the northeastern vicinity of the state as my focus points. As I accumulated data, I narrowed my focus point into the Warren, Washington and Essex County regions as a stopping point due to their highest volume of reports out of the state.

Maps, books, photos, and videos will provide an outlet to join in on the search. Collaboration, high-end equipment, and sighting-report maps will also assist, and boots on the ground on a wide array of properties will help bring our studies out into the light.

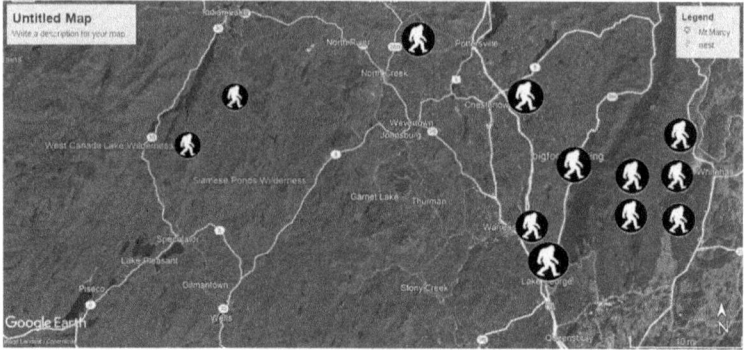

NY sightings map

One incident tells the story of a man who thought the splashing and thunking were from a beaver in the water until the rocks started hitting very close to where he was standing. They were the size of a basketball. One struck the man's vehicle, but the story did not detail the possible reactions of the insurance adjuster.

Eyewitnesses describe these hominids as having a foul odor. This could explain the report of a highly pungent, neglected-human smell in a wilderness area near Moody Pond.

One woman was washing dishes when she looked up through her kitchen window. She found herself staring into a hairy surprised face only a foot from her own. Apparently, it was a comedic moment where both of them screamed, and the skunk ape ran away. In a typical trailer configuration, her home was mounted on cement blocks. For this intruder to be face-to-face with her, he was at least eight feet tall.

There are many Bigfoot-related stories going back as far as two hundred years that are documented in newspaper articles that are referred to as "hairy wild men" that roam our forests.

Massena resident Michael Guimond was driving home on County Route 37 at about 11:30 p.m. on June 20 when he spotted what he believes to be a Sasquatch. "Something bipedal ran across the road within fifty feet of my car; this thing was extremely fast," Guimond said. "I was going sixty; it crossed the road from right to left in less than a second. It was not a deer. I've seen plenty of deer. This thing was brown or gray, shaggy and had arms and legs that moved in a circular motion." Guimond posted on Facebook about his sighting the same night, causing a slew of stories from other people within the area having the same experiences. "I lived there in 2011, and I started walking my dog outside at night around 8:30," Aric Lauzon said. "The woods at the back of my house went on for miles and miles. I was out there a couple nights, and I kept hearing a loud screaming noise. It sounded like nothing I have ever heard before in my life. It sounds like a mix between an elephant and a bear; it goes right through you; it's defining."

In the summer of 1996, a group of friends were camping in the Pine Pond area, at the base of Mount Ampersand. As dusk fell, they were fishing from a canoe. The two were chatting, and the witness was scanning the northern bank of the lake, a place they were familiar with, except for a strange shape on the edge of the wood line, about fifty yards away. His friend immediately saw it, too. Both recalled later that it reminded them of a black bear standing broadside. They began to row cautiously toward it. The friend whispered, "It's a bear," but then the shape stood up, revealing that it "had been crouching there on its feet like a catcher from a baseball team."

As it was standing upright, they estimated it to be at least seven feet tall with dark brown hair, with a face that was fleshy around the upper cheeks. Dark eyes were clearly visible and "had a brightness about them." Both agreed they saw the creature moving its head and hands and that it looked at them for long seconds, maybe as long as ten seconds, with its head tilted up as though sniffing the air. The sound of snapping twigs some fifty feet behind it made the creature spring into action. It turned to its side, then checked on the canoe before spinning completely around, "darting into the wood line like a cat."

The two friends floated in the canoe, debating on the wisdom of paddling to shore to look for tracks. The witness's wishes to get away were overridden by the curiosity of his companion, but upon investigation, they did find two markings in the sand, rather blurred from the pivoting movements of its feet. The witness found the whole experience extremely upsetting, even though the creature did not act threatening, and every sound that night kept them awake. The people who did not have the experience claimed they saw a bear. "It was no bear."

The FBI files reveal a conversation between one man who pushed the agency to test the existence of Bigfoot. In August 1976, Peter C. Bryne, then the director of the Bigfoot Information Center and Exhibit based in The Dalles, Oregon, wrote to the FBI, asking the agency to confirm or deny that they had tested hair samples of Bigfoot. Bryne attached to his letter two newspaper articles that state the FBI has tested hairs suspected to belong to a Bigfoot, and tests indicated the hair did not match any known creature. FBI assistant director Jay Cochran Jr. wrote back to Byrne saying the tests cited in the articles never happened. In November 1976, the FBI agreed to test the hair samples Byrne had. The FBI concluded that the hair samples thought to belong to Bigfoot came from a member of "deer family origin," according to the records. More on locations will be discussed in the following chapters.

KINDERHOOK

Less than a hundred miles south of Whitehall sits the town of Kinderhook, which has a long history of Bigfoot sightings. During my investigations into the Whitehall area, I was made aware of the small town by a local eyewitness who informed me of a rash of strange creature reports that took place in the early 1980s. This town was mostly famous for its haunted history of ghosts and headless horsemen and a dead president, Martin Van Buren, who was born and buried here. But spirits and lost souls are not the only mystery residing here in Kinderhook. Reports of tall, hairy, elusive creatures going back several decades have been witnessed by many of the locals.

In December of 1978, two local cousins in their early teens discovered a strange set of tracks that appeared to have only three toes in the snow in a patch of swampland and forest. The two cousins decided to follow the tracks in the snow, which seemed to abruptly end mid snow. One of the boys photographed the tracks and sent a copy to the *Hudson River Chronicle*, which promptly lost the photos. The boys were stumped over how or where the creature went.

I find it interesting that a large hairy hominid living in the forest will leave tracks with only three toes. However, this is not the first claim of that enigma. In the early 1970s, while Momo was stomping around Missouri, an identical monster appeared one state down, in Miller County, Arkansas. From 1971 to 1974, the Fouke Monster, a seven-and-a half-foot, hairy, humanlike creature that smelled like skunk and rotting flesh, was reportedly seen in southwestern Arkansas. Both creatures appeared to have possessed three-toed footprints. The Ohio grassman and the skunk ape in Florida have also been famous for leaving three-toed tracks in their path. As I take a deeper look into the areas in which all four of these hominids reside, I start to see their environment is a swampy or marshy land as opposed to your traditional forest or mountainous region.

Going as far back as the 1960s, there have been six different eyewitness accounts of what was described as a "floating, blob-like creature" in the woods of Kinderhook, New York. There was even a sighting as recently as 2017.

The first encounter was reported by a ten-year-old boy, who was playing in the woods with his seven-year-old cousin. When at the age of ten years old (1962), he and his cousin, who was seven at the time, were out in the woods behind his house when they both heard a really high-pitched whistle noise. The young boy said they went looking for the source of the sound and eventually spotted what looked to be a white, formless figure that seemed to leer at them, although "it had no eyes that I could see." The two youths quickly ran back to their house. A couple of years went by without any new encounters. But then a mysterious man claimed to have spotted something similar when he was hiking through the woods, saying a "big white blob" was floating toward him. He was reportedly so shaken by the experience that he jumped a pond that was six feet across.

The man returned hours later with a friend, looking for the creature, and this time both were armed with shovels and pitchforks. When they both saw it again, they were so startled that they dropped their gear and went running.

Personal note: On occasion we get reports of Bigfoot having three toes, primarily in the southeast, and five toes in the rest of North America. And many researchers have been curious as to why we would have this variation. There are roughly 260 known monkey species, and as far as I know, only one has anything but a five-five finger-toe count; that is the spider monkey with a four-five finger-toe count. And all apes do have a five-five finger-toe count. If there were one known case of a Bigfoot having three toes, I could chalk that up to a genetic disorder; however, a whole demographic displaying this trait makes me wonder. Could this be a case of some time ago the Bigfoot population in this area was hunted or brought to the verge of extinction, and a genetic anomaly has been passed along by the select few that carried this trait and passed it along?

The theory of evolution by natural selection was first formulated in Charles Darwin's book *On the Origin of Species* published in 1859. In his book, Darwin describes how organisms evolve over generations through the inheritance of physical or behavioral traits, as *National Geographic* explains. The theory starts with the premise that within a population, there is variation in traits, such as beak shape in one of the finches Darwin studied.

According to the theory, individuals with traits that enable them to adapt to their environments will help them survive and have more offspring, which will inherit those traits. Individuals with less adaptive traits will less frequently survive to pass them on. Over time, the traits that enable species to survive and reproduce will become more frequent in the population, and the population will change, or evolve, according to Biomed central. Through natural selection, Darwin suggested, genetically diverse species could arise from a common ancestor. Darwin did not know the mechanism by which traits were passed on, according to *National Geographic*. He did not know about genetics, the mechanism by which genes encode for certain traits and those traits are passed from one generation to the next. He also did not know about genetic mutation, which is the source of natural variation. But future research by geneticists provided the mechanism and additional evidence for evolution.

Darwin also speculated about how natural selection could cause a land mammal to turn into a whale. As a hypothetical example, Darwin used North American black bears (*Ursus americanus*), which were known to catch insects by swimming in the water with their mouths open, according to the Darwin Project. But a three-toed hominid living on the East Coast in marsh or swamp areas raise some questions of the possibility of mutations.

Mutations can be caused by random errors in DNA replication or repair, or by chemical or radiation damage, according to Nature Education. Usually, mutations are either harmful or neutral, but in rare instances, a mutation might prove beneficial to the organism. If so, it will become more prevalent in the next generation and spread throughout the population.

It wasn't long after this rash of reports when a grandmother looked out her kitchen window one early morning in 1978 and saw what appeared to be a large creature curled up in a resting position on her lawn. Due to the fact that it was in the early dawn of the morning, she couldn't see it clearly, but it looked strange enough to her that she didn't report the incident for fear of ridicule. "I didn't tell anyone," she later said, "because I was afraid people would cart me away somewhere. It was only afterward, when other people said they had seen the same things, that I talked about it." She later described it as "a big black thing curled up down at the end of the lawn," and she found tracks in the snow. "I had my garbage in a green bag, the same as I have on the back porch now, only I had it out there at the corner of the house, and it used to be taken up and set down in the lawn down there, and things were taken out of it.

"The bag wasn't torn. Someone was untying the knot in the bag, like a human would do. But the food was taken out, and just as though a person took it out, nothing like an animal would do, and I kept wondering about that because if the dogs get in it, it would be all over the place. And yet it wasn't. It was very neat."

Soon after that incident, the grandmother received a call from her neighbors claiming to have experienced a similar incident with something stealing their trash that they had stored in their shed. They also found one of their empty trash bags up in a tree. The grandmother also noted that the creature seemed to appear and disappear. "One minute it's there, and the next minute it's gone. And we have seen tracks leading somewhere, and even the tracks seem to stop, and you don't see them anymore."

The grandmother also noted that there was no noticeable odor to the creature during any of her sightings. One other interesting piece to the case is that three dead rabbits were found in a snowbank at the top of Cushing's Hill, as if they were being stored away for the winter. No footprints were found around the area, and because it was in a very remote spot, it added more mystery to the surrounding case. Strangely enough, most of the unexplained activity seemed to be centered around Cushing's Hill, including UFO reports.

Approximately one calendar year later in December, activity started back up again. As the grandson was setting traps near the creek in Cushing's Hill, he spotted four large creatures crossing the creek and headed into the woods. The grandson ran back home to tell his grandmother what he had seen.

Days after the sighting, two other locals decided to set out and canvas the wooded area and maybe see what they could discover, only to come up empty. In April of 1980, another eyewitness was returning from Albany late one night on Route 9 when she spotted something in her headlights that she described as seven and a half feet in height with reddish brown hair. "It looked like a highly evolved ape," the witness claimed. The woman slowed her car as she watched it walk across the road and into the cornfield, where it disappeared into the night.

Many reports of up to three at once were seen near Kinderhook Creek the previous year. Tracks were found, and vocalizations were heard emanating from the deeply wooded creek in the late night hours all through 1981.

In November of that year, a local teenager and his two cousins were walking up a side road towards Cushing's Hill to meet up with a female friend who lived nearby. As they traveled farther up the road, they began to hear noises as if something large was moving through the woods, pacing them from both sides of the wooded road. Moments later, five figures conversed in the middle of the remote road. The figures were described as very tall, with no visible necks and cone-shaped heads. As the teen turned to mention it to his cousins, they had already frighteningly taken off down the road. Ironically, as the girlfriend of the teenage witness was coming to meet up with him from the other direction, she saw one of the hairy creatures reaching into the garbage can near her house, taking out food and eating it.

In June of 1981, the crew from *PM Magazine*, the nationally syndicated TV show, set out to do a segment of the program of what they officially deemed as "the Kinderhook

Creature." During their visit, several three-toed tracks were found in the woods near the grandmother's house, measuring fourteen inches in length and approximately seven inches in width. The *PM* film crew were quite impressed with this find, so much that the film crew decided to stay around and shoot a segment that evening in the vicinity of Cushing's Hill. As luck would have it, it was also a full moon that night. Just as the *PM* crew was setting up their equipment, they began to hear three distinct noises coming from the swamp. The first sounds were described as "monkey chatter" similar to the Ron Morehead recordings. The second sound was a very high-pitched scream. And the third was described as the sound of a baby crying.

During the summer of 1981, a family just outside of Kinderhook lived at the far end of a dead-end road, bordered on all sides by woods. The family claimed to have had dealings with a big black hairy-looking beast that they described as "it only came out at night," and their two dogs would cowardly hide in the corner of the house when "it" came around. They had a large barrel of fish left outside, and one morning they found the barrel had been lifted and put into the woods down by a nearby creek bed. Nearly all the fish had been taken out. They had some extremely large tracks measuring over sixteen inches long leading away from the barrel. Several investigators from different agencies investigated the incident, including the New York State Department of Environmental Conservation, who remarked: "If those are bear tracks, it's a real monster." Since the incident, the family has refused to come forward with any new information.

In May of 1981, a former employee of the Ichabod Crane school system was fishing late one afternoon near a dam not far from Kinderhook. He felt something looking at him, he remarked, and when he looked up, he observed a creature looking at him from across Kinderhook Creek, approximately twenty yards away. The witness described the creature as about eight feet tall, with long hair on its head and short hair on its body that was a reddish brown color. It had small red eyes, and he also noticed that its fingernails were black. Both he and the creature spent a couple of minutes staring at each other; the creature then casually walked off into the woods where it emerged from. The witness did not pursue it.

During apple season in 1982 in Kinderhook, there were a number of sightings of a white Bigfoot reported. There were also reports of one in the town of Kinderhook near an apple orchard. Reports of the white Bigfoot said it had been seen running through the apple orchard by a local farmer. There were also several sightings of the white Bigfoot that winter in the Chatham area.

During the summer of 1982, two local cousins decided to set bait for the creature in hope to possibly catch or obtain evidence of its existence. A modified bird feeder with its side removed was used on their lawn with foods not used in attracting birds. Various lures were used, but "it" always took the steak. Hotdogs and chicken always went untouched, but steak and other red meat was always taken. Surprisingly enough, footprints were never found despite the flour spread on the ground area around the bird feeder. A box of pizza was left out one night next to the bird feeder. The next day the box was found with claw marks on the outside, down in the bushes at the far end of their property, but the pizza inside wasn't eaten. There was a great deal of evidence that supports that this creature feeds off red meat, including rabbits that were found frozen one year in a snowbank near Cushing's Hill. Ironically, the father saw something near his birdfeeder around dusk, standing out under a large willow tree in his backyard.

The existence of these beings has sparked more questions than answers. The controversy between a flesh and blood creature or a paranormal entity remains debatable at best. However, the question most asked is, where do they live, or where do they go? The area around Cushing's Hill provides plenty of dense underbrush, swampland and sinkholes for creatures that live nomadic lives and rest wherever they can.

2017

The most recent encounter was in 2017, when two Kinderhook residents, Owen Farley and Anthony Malanowski, spotted the "blob" on a walk. The two men said there was a noticeable drop in temperature directly before the sighting, followed by a high-pitched screech. The two eyewitnesses described "a white blob, around seven feet tall" come out of the woods and float towards them. Both men ran away in fear. Speculations of extraterrestrial activity were at play. Interestingly enough, reports of UFO activity in the night sky were also reported to the MUFON database.

The creature is said to be somewhere between amorphous and bell-shaped. It is white and has no distinguishing features – and no distinguishable face. Rather than walk, it floats without touching the ground. Across the sightings, there does not seem to be a uniform size to the creature, with one witness claiming it was as tall as seven feet, with other descriptions claiming it was only a few feet in height – insinuating that there may be more than one of these things floating around Kinderhook.

Theories:
There have been a few theories thrown around when it comes to the Kinderhook blob. As usual, they range from believable to utterly strange and unusual. First, the obvious – that this is some sort of prank that people were pulling on each other in the '60s (and maybe '70s, depending on when that third encounter took place). Then the perpe-

trator of the 2017 sighting heard about those sightings and decided to bring it back. This would mostly explain the variances in sizes and shapes of the blobs. However, it does not explain the sudden drop in temperature or even the gliding across wide expanses.

The next theory I have seen in my research is that the blob is some sort of ghost. Obviously, there is no way to prove or disprove this, but I think this theory would explain the temperature drops and the variance in the physical representations of the creature. If you believe in spirits, then you know the possibility of the paranormal. Finally, maybe it really is some sort of creature that is running around the woods in Upstate New York that has gone mostly undiscovered. Who's to say what's possible and not when it comes to the cryptozoological field?

1983

In May of 1983, at the corner of Route 203 in Kinderhook, a mother and her daughter were making a right-hand turn at the cow pasture at Route 203 and State Farm Road in Valatie when they witnessed a large, hairy, manlike beast at least seven feet in height. The witnesses describe it to be getting up from what appeared to be a crouching position into a standing position. The driver stopped the car to observe and noticed that it glanced their way, then took off in the opposite direction through the cow pasture. The witnesses describe the creature's hair as a long light brown. The hair covered its face with the exception of the eyes and mouth.

1998

On a cool moonlit morning in August of 1998, two couples were driving on Route 203 at approximately 2 a.m., when they pulled their car to the side of the road to urinate. "Chris" returned to the vehicle, and when he turned on his high beams, he noticed a huge figure standing about twenty yards away. The figure was between seven to eight feet tall, part human, part animal, and had a flat face that swung in an exaggerated motion. Covered in long brown hair, Chris describes, "it stood perfectly still for a minute and then grunted at us. Then it turned and walked away. It didn't move like a man. It kind of swaggered back and forth, like it lunged each leg forward when it walked."

LAKE GEORGE

Lake George, nicknamed the Queen of American Lakes, is a long, narrow lake located at the southeast base of the Adirondack Mountains, in the northeastern portion of New York. It lies within the upper region of the Great Appalachian Valley and drains all the way northward into Lake Champlain and the St. Lawrance River. The lake is situated along the historical natural Amerindian path between the valleys of the Hudson and St. Lawrence Rivers, and so lies on the direct land route between Albany, NY, and Montreal, Canada. The lake extends about 32.2 miles on a north-south axis, is 187 feet deep, and ranges from one to three miles in width, presenting a significant barrier to east-west travel.

New York is number five on most lists of Bigfoot sightings by state, and heavily wooded Hudson valley is a hotbed of them. *Hudson Valley* magazine listed sightings at Nuclear Lake in Pawling, Stissing Mountain in Pine Plains, Peekamoose in Ulster County, Bear Mountain in Rockland, the ice caves in Ellenville, and Greenwood Lake in Orange County, just to name a few.

JUNE 17 OF 2015

At around midafternoon, two eyewitnesses were boating along the eastern shore of Lake George, NY. At approximately 43 degrees north and traveling around 5 mph, there was a point of land opposite the rocky outcrop on the east bay. The couple simultaneously witnessed what they described as a " very large black animate object" about 140 yards away that seemed to quickly raise an arm from its side to a horizontal position, then turn away and move back and to the side behind a nearby clump of trees. They then spun the boat around for a better view. Their first impression was that it possibly could have been a black bear. As they observed the movement in the object, they realized that it wasn't a bear. During their short duration in observing the object, they were confident in believing that it was a hairy hominid of unknown origin.

The couple then continued on to Fox Island, which was about two hundred yards from their sighting and approximately fifty feet from shore. The couple eventually got a charcoal grill going to cook their traditional meals. As the two were eating, they both suddenly had the eerie feeling of being watched. They both quickly finished up and loaded their gear back onto the boat and left the area.

The couple returned to the area on July 6 of 2015, by boat, with his brother, who happened to be a photographer, interested in investigating the mainland. As they ventured into the area where the creature had been sighted, they noticed a small seasonal stream that flowed into the lake. No tracks or footprints were found. Later, they installed a trail cam in the hopes of catching an image of the being, but the trail cam yielded zero results.

SABBATH DAY POINT

Another sighting in Warren County involving two men in a canoe took place on the shore of Lake George in an area known as Deer Leap in the spring of 1990. Deer Leap is an area of boulders and cliffs rising to six hundred feet above the shoreline. Making my assessment from the story and the sketch that was submitted, I would say that this may not have been a Bigfoot, but possibly an undiscovered reptilian mammal.

When the two witnesses saw it, they described it as brownish in color, about the size of a small man and very thin and standing straight up on the shore with its arms at its sides. Its body was facing south, and it was looking down the shoreline. Suddenly, it then turned its head directly towards the two men and stared at them very intently. As the two watched it while it was watching them, they began paddling parallel to the shore about two hundred feet out from the object in question. "It had a strange look on its face, almost like a crazed grin. It looked almost like a giant lemur." The two men continued to watch it as it was standing next to an old dead pine tree, as it climbed sloth-like up the tree about twenty feet to the first large limb and then onto the crook of a branch. They paddled back around and approached it a second time; it cocked its head directly towards them. "After about a minute, it turned its face downward into its body, and it looked like it became part of the tree. It blended in so perfectly it looked just like a lump in the crook of the branch. You would never have known that it was there unless you saw it move." The eyewitness submitted this sketch with his report.

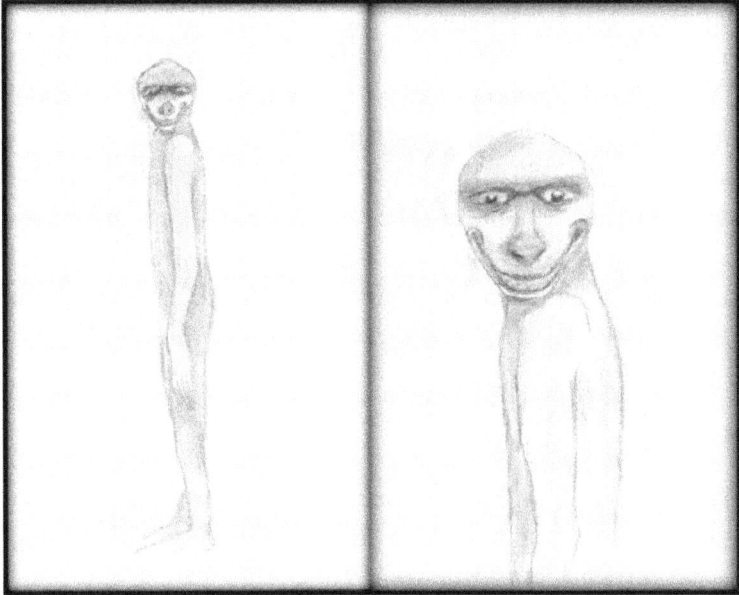

Update. 2009. Several years later, two girls, one of them being
a lifeguard at a nearby YMCA camp, saw something they
described as a "monkey boy" jumping on and off a wall.
According to the two eyewitnesses, this creature in question
had a small tail that wasn't mentioned in the previous case.

*Personal note: If there's one of these little guys, then there must be
more than one in order to sustain an adequate breeding population.
However, population size to maintain genetic diversity isn't the only
thing at play. Location and movement of genetics is probably more
important than actual numbers. The accounts of a species in a family
unit would also play into genetic diversity and inbreeding.*

MARCH 31, 2006

"I was hiking alone two miles south of Sabbath Day Point just
off Route 9 north. I was near a small body of water when I
heard odd sounds about three hundred yards away. The
sounds were from a large creature. They were 'singsong' in
pattern and unlike anything I have ever heard. The creature

appeared to be talking to itself, as there was only one creature. It did not sound angry and lasted for about two minutes.
The sound changed in pitch and fluctuation. I was not scared
but did leave quickly. I have since studied sounds of coyotes
and found no similarities at all. There were no yelps, barks or
growls. I cannot duplicate the sounds. It's like nothing I have
ever heard in the woods or elsewhere. My wife and I went
back two weeks later and found no signs of anything out of
the norm."

MAY 2001

Near Sabbath Day Point in the Lake George region. "I am not
much of an outdoorsman, so bear with me on the descriptions, terrain, etc. After researching this area, I saw there
have been a few sightings in this area. Which is why I'm
reaching out to you. It was approximately 3:30 a.m. when I
awoke. Two friends and I were in a tent. Five other friends
had a cabin about one mile from us. We'd decided to 'rough it'
as much as we could. I went outside the tent to make a phone
call on my cell phone (I know, really roughing it); my brother
gets off work at 3 a.m. I needed to call him because I needed a
ride in the morning. I was about twenty feet from the tent.
My friend yelled, 'I'm trying to sleep,' so I walked another
twenty feet from the tent.

"After I spoke to my brother, I saw the time was 3:48. I
then went to go to the bathroom. That was when I heard a
noise coming from in front of me. I was easily scared, as I am
not used to being in the woods very often. I stepped back a
little, and I saw, approximately sixty feet in front of me, a
figure coming up a slight incline in the terrain. My first
thought was, 'Ok, a bear in front of me; run.' As I went to
run, I noticed it had turned slightly, and the one main charac-
teristic I noticed was no snout like a bear would have. More

like a human face although I couldn't see features, but more of an outline. This really scared me.

"I ran to the tent and told my friends. They were sure it was a bear, and we waited ten minutes before going back to the cabin. I realized that this 'thing' that I saw had a human shape. I got a look at it for maybe five seconds. And like I said, I'm not much of an outdoorsman and probably wouldn't know a bear from an ape in the woods. But I saw something unusual. It looked like a human hairy man walking up a hill (fairly blunt but the best way I could describe it). I was thinking it could be a bear on its hind legs, but it wasn't staggering. It was WALKING. The thoughts of Bigfoot didn't enter my mind until a few days later, and I have to say I don't believe in such tales that I see in supermarket tabloids. But whatever it was, it sure was a unique experience."

MAY 2009

"I was spending a few days in Lake George during time off from work and decided to do some fishing around the area of Sabbath Day Point with just myself and my dog. We spent the morning along the shore to do some fishing; then we went out to explore some trails nearby. After about twenty minutes or so, I heard my dog barking and growling. I figured that he stirred up a deer, but when I looked in the direction of the ruckus, I noticed a dark hairy creature bobbing up and down in the thickets. I stopped fishing and moved closer to get a better look and noticed that the dog stopped barking. Suddenly, I heard a loud yelp from the dog, and the creature stood up. The best I could tell was that this thing was about seven to eight feet tall and had dark matted hair. I could only see the body from the chest up because the rest of the body was obscured by the weeds and thickets. I stood completely still and could hear a series of tick sounds while observing this creature walk slowly through the thickets towards the woods. My dog then ran back in the direction towards me at full sprint and continued past me down the trail. I went running after him in pursuit and finally caught up to him at the end of the trail where I had parked my truck. I noticed he was quivering and shaking with his tail between his legs. For the safety of my dog, I decided to pack up and head home that same day."

Personal note: Animals reacting in fear when faced with these creatures is not an isolated incident. There have been hundreds of cases where dogs of all different breeds, including trained guard dogs, have cowered in fear when confronted by them. Theories speculated the possibility of the use of infrasound. Studies have shown infrasound, sometimes referred to as low-frequency sound, is sound that is lower in frequency than 20 Hz (or cycles per second), the normal limit of human hearing. Whales, elephants, hippopotamuses, rhinos, giraffes, and tigers are known to use infrasound to communicate over distances. One study has suggested that infrasound may cause feelings of awe or extreme fear in humans or other animals.

AUGUST 2001

In the area of Split Rock Road, three married couples decided to go camping at Jabes Pond near Sabbath Day Point. Evidently, there were no other campers in that area. The witnesses claim they stayed up till 2:30 a.m. next to their campfire before the females went to bed for the night. By 3 a.m., four out of the six campers decided to turn in for the night, leaving a husband and wife by the fire. Their tents were set up by the lakeshore approximately two feet from the water.

"As the husband climbed into bed next to his wife, they heard the sound of water splashing near the tent at close range. The wife sat up and said, "Something is out there." The couple quietly listened, and within minutes they heard the sound of branches breaking from behind their tent. As the husband was in the tent lying on his back, looking up, he observed an elbow dragged down the side of the tent, followed by five thuds of something running away. From his observation, he estimated the intruder had to have been well over six feet or taller. Neither the husband nor the wife got an accurate look at the individual, and when they asked their fellow camping partners, they claim to have slept through it.

JULY 1992

Witnesses describe the occurrences happening between the hours of 10:30 to 3 a.m., lasting from one to four minutes. "The first sounds were that of a whirling shrill whistling, then a deep thumping and with the lung capacity of a horse being slaughtered, along with various chattering and screams; to hear this once is not to want to hear it again. At some point in the night, my two-year-old daughter woke crying. She said the creature woke her up. But it kept coming back almost every night. It sounded about two hundred feet away, while looking out the windows with a small flashlight, but I could not see anything. I really did not want to see what it was. I was too terrified. Our cabin was located between Route 9N and approximately seventy-five feet from the lake. The mountain directly behind us was Bloomer Mountain. Sometimes the sounds started far away on top of the mountain. Then within a minute the sound was coming from the road area. There may have been two of them calling to each other. We don't own this property any longer. This is one of the most beautiful areas of the world and not heavily populated."

Personal note: In my years of researching these encounters, children seem to play an important role in a number of these encounters. It is my experience that they take a high interest in our young. There are a very high number of reported encounters involving children in all areas of North America. Such as, looking in windows, showing them-selves, etc. Are these creatures merely curious and confident getting closer to humans that are obviously not a threat? Or does the child represent an easy meal? Some children have been stolen and carried away while others are mysteriously brought back to camp after getting lost. Some children who lived to report the encounter describe intense fear while others describe only curiosity and the excitement of finding a new playmate.

BUCK MOUNTAIN

JULY 2000

"My wife and I were off about half a mile to the trail on Buck Mountain to take some photos since she works as a model, and I wanted to get some pictures of her by the creek. There were two other cars parked at the trailhead when we went into the trail and signed the login registration at the trailhead.

"We had been at the location for thirty minutes when we heard a very deep sound, almost roaring sound, from a very large mammal. I am an experienced backpacker and had years of experience in Boy Scouts and have had many encounters with bears and on occasion have had to take food bags away from a very large bear that stole a hiker's food near Avalanche Pass in the high peaks. I have heard bobcats and coydogs, and this was no animal that I have ever heard, including a possible Bigfoot sighting I had nearly ten years ago. The sound was so distinct, so low, almost a cross between a scream and a growling sound. I had never heard anything like this in all my life. It made the hair stand up on the back of my neck. I have never been as frightened in all my life. I tried to keep my cool with my wife, who frightens easily.

"The sound came closer and closer and was coming from the other side of the creek from the trail. It made this blood-curdling scream/yell at least seven times as it approached us, and at one point it was about twenty-five feet away. As it came through the woods, we could hear large branches breaking, and we could tell it was starting to circle us. The sounds stopped, but we could just feel it looking at us. We were in total fear, and we quickly gathered our things and ran down the trail; the whole time we could hear this very large animal tracking us to our right side along the creek."

JUNE 2017

"This happened late at night at around 2:30 a.m. I was camping out in Buck Mountain in the area of Shelving Rock Road, campsite #10. I arrived there at around 7 p.m. and set up my tent for the night. I made a campfire at around 9:30–10:00 and fried some steak and beans while enjoying the solitude of the wilderness and some downtime to myself. There were other campers in the nearby campsites, maybe three or four other cars on that road. At around midnight I went to bed for the night.

"At some point in the middle of the night, I was wakened by the sound of something going through my cooler and camping gear. Apparently, I put my trust in nature by leaving my stuff outside for the night. As I sat up in my tent, I could hear something rummaging through my property. I quietly peeked my head out of my tent zipper, and I couldn't believe what I was seeing. It looked like a person about five feet tall, covered in dark hair, going through my cooler. 'It' was taking things (cans of food and beer cans) out of my cooler and holding them up to its face and smelling them, then tossing them over its shoulder. I could tell it wasn't a person, it was making grunting and snorting sounds, and its head had an unusual cone shape to the top of its skull.

"As I looked over to the left of it, I noticed an even bigger one standing next to a tree, looking directly at me. This one had to have been about nine feet tall and built like a power-lifter. I ducked back into my tent and sat motionless. I was frightened shitless. About an hour later the noises stopped. But I didn't dare come out and look until daylight the next morning. When the sun finally came up, I could see what a mess they'd made in my campsite. All of my canned goods were scattered everywhere, along with my cans of beer and camping equipment. The only items they took were three of my raw steaks that I kept in a plastic bag that I had in the cooler. I packed up and left that morning and didn't want to take a chance on another incident with them again."

Personal note: He was in the right area for that kind of encounter. It appears that that area in the months of May, June and July have the most reports, indicating a migration route through that mountain. It was also my suspicion that the aroma of his campfire steak may have possibly alerted the creatures to his campsite. His descriptions of the juvenile and adult Sasquatch are consistent with what other eyewitnesses have described. Upon corresponding with him through email, he did not take photos of the area, nor did he notice or observe any footprints in the surrounding area. However, late night encounters in that general area are not uncommon.

AUGUST 2015

"I grew up in Albany, NY, and lived there all my life. I work as a consultant for a small company. In late August of 2015, myself and my two sons (ages twelve and fourteen) decided to take a trip up to Lake George for a five-day vacation. Our first couple of days we spent on the lake and around town, buying gifts and enjoying what the tourist area had to offer. We then decided to explore the mountains and trails around the vicinity.

"We came upon some trails via my GPS and chose to explore Inman Pond. We parked on the side of the dirt road and signed the logbook that was at the beginning of the trail-head. We proceeded up the trail and followed the trail signs to Inman Pond. During our hike, my oldest son had the feeling that we were being followed. I didn't see anyone else on the trail, so I assured him it was his imagination.

"As we approached the pond, a rock came out from my right side and hit a nearby tree. I looked in the direction it was thrown but didn't see anyone. We all stopped and looked at each other and paused. As we walked another ten yards, another rock about the size of a softball hit the tree in front of us. I thought to myself that whoever threw that rock had to have one hell of an arm to toss a rock like that. At that point, I felt fear for the safety of myself and my kids. I then guided them back down the trail to head back to the car.

"As we walked back down the trail, we could hear foot-steps pacing us in the woods on our left side. When we stopped, it would stop. And when we started walking, we heard footsteps, and a few times we heard the sound of tree branches snapping. Whoever was following us was very stealthy at not being seen, but not at being silent. It's almost as if they wanted us to hear them.

"We arrived back at the car, and my two kids asked me what was following us. I really wasn't sure who or what was in the woods, but the safety of my kids comes first. Has anyone else experienced something like that out there? Maybe someone didn't want us there."

Personal note: Rock throwing is a commonly known behavior among encounters with these creatures. The interpretation of just what this behavior means may differ based on some factors. There seems to be a couple different scenarios when it comes to rock throwing. There are many reports of Bigfoot throwing small pebbles at researchers or at people hiking. The general consensus seems to be that this behavior, of throwing very small size rocks, is more of a curiosity type of thing and that the creature is not out to hurt or injure the person and is perhaps just monitoring the reaction. It is also thought that on some occasion they will use the small pebbles to kind of move people out of an area. Then there are reports of much larger rocks being thrown. Some of these reports describe the rocks to be bigger than a basketball. Some boaters have had large sized rocks come flying and splashing into the water in other parts of the country. It would seem that these larger stones are of a more aggressive nature. That this is a stern warning to get out of the area. I would think most would heed this warning. Even though most see these types of events as being more aggressive, motives for this could possibly be if a person has got too close to say the clan in general, or maybe too close to very young Bigfoot. Of course, most of this is all just speculation based on the witnesses and researchers I have talked to about this subject. There are other activities with rocks that are attributed to Bigfoot. Things like rocks stacks and rock clacking. Rock stacks are also done by hikers, so this makes it harder to discern who actually made them. Some rock stacks are very large, but it is important to realize that sometime Native American's stacked rocks in this manner. These large stacks also were done by surveyors as a way to mark property.

BRANT LAKE

OCTOBER 1992

Brant Lake. At approximately 6 a.m., a motorist was driving to work near Brant Lake when something from the right side of the road emerged from the woods and onto the road, forcing the driver to stop his car. The driver paused for a few seconds to process what he was seeing. The object in front of him he describes as seven to eight feet tall, with white or light gray hair from head to toe. The creature was standing about ten to twelve feet in front of his vehicle, directly in the head-lights, giving the driver a perfect view. "It" was standing facing the left side of the road with a slight left twist in its body. The eyewitness describes, "We stared at each other for what seemed to be minutes, but I can't say for sure how long. I had absolutely no fear of this creature; it seemed to have a sad demeanor. This creature made no sound at all. I don't have any reason to believe it was male or female. Needless to say, I have carried my camera ever since, but I believe that it was a once-in-a-lifetime incident."

Personal note: Brant Lake has been an area of strange activity for decades including UFO activity, Bigfoot reports and strange disappearances. Recently on November 15, 2015, an 82 year old ex-para-trooper, walked into the woods south of Brant Lake in NY State, to hunt for deer with some of his longtime friends and was never seen again. No sign of him or his belongings ever turned up, including a rifle and walkie-talkie, despite a large search of the area, Unusually the FBI was even involved in the investigation. This is a strange and puzzling hunting disappearance.

SARANAC LAKE

For hundreds of years Saranac Lake has been steeped in mysteries, from haunted places to UFO activity in the sky above, and reports of Bigfoot in the nearby wooded areas. The mystery over what's flying around in the skies of Saranac Lake has the attention of UFO investigators.

A Saranac Lake woman claims she saw large waves rippling out in a swirling motion on the lake. Moments later, she claims to have seen a large hairy hominid, brown in color, walking away from the lake, headed into the woods. And for many thousands of years Native Americans freely traversed the domed mountain range that serves in present times as the border between Canada and the United States. Then, like now, it was a formidable and at times extremely inhospitable environment, suitable for hunting, trapping or fishing, but little else. So no one ever thought to make it a permanent residence.

The name "Adirondack" is in fact a bastardized version of the Mohawk word *Ratironaks*, which translated means "they eat trees." The full force of that translation is somewhat lost on us today though, because it was a deeply derogatory term that the Mohawks used to describe the Algonquian-speaking tribes, whom they claimed dined on tree buds and bark whenever better food became scarce. History has shown that fate has been unkind to all Native American peoples, so it is therefore impossible now to verify either the superiority of the Mohawk way of life or the Algonquians' lowliness. But the historical grudges and insults of one tribe lobbed against the other are probably best dismissed as amounting to nothing more than ordinary cultural bias, such as has plagued every civilization since the beginning of time.

MAY 2022

At approximately 3:20 in the afternoon, a seventy-nine-year-old retired land surveyor was driving east on Dugway Road in Chesterfield, NY, in Essex County when he observed a tall black hairy hominid about three hundred feet away, standing on the left side of the road next to a large white pine tree. The eyewitness states, "It was gone down the hill. I stopped, got out, and searched for prints or maybe catch a smell.

Found nothing; smelled nothing. That creature bolted so fast downslope towards the Ausable River through heavy woods, the sighting lasted a few seconds." He described it as being black in color, and he was able to notice its long arms as it turned away to evade the area of the approaching motorist.

Personal note: I think that was very brave of him to stop and get out to observe the area for footprints moments after seeing such a creature. Afternoon encounters are very rare but do occur. I observed the area where the sighting took place, and Ausable River is just north of Dugway Road, and Augur Lake is less than one mile south of his encounter. Also observed is that both sides of Dugway Road are heavily forested, giving the possibility of wildlife activity in the surrounding vicinity.

OCTOBER 2022

"On our way back to Paul Smith's College from our dendrology lab, I noticed a large figure out the window by the powerlines. At first I thought it was a large man in a fur coat because I could see its arms, legs, head, and torso, but this creature was much too big to be a man, and the fur seemed to be covering its entire body. It was about one-third the size of the telephone poles (about thirty-foot poles) that made up the powerlines, and was walking close enough to them for me to have a good comparison. That would make this thing about eight to ten feet tall, roughly. It had its back to me and seemed to be casually strolling north along the path the powerlines went. It was moving slowly and didn't seem spooked by any of the traffic on the road. But it was a good 100–125 yards down the powerlines, so maybe that's why it wasn't spooked."

SUMMER 2018

"We bought a house that was unoccupied for almost six years; the previous owner had a fully stocked woodshed at the rear of the six-acre property, which pretty much butts up to state forest land/a wildlife preserve. Usually late at night we'd hear screaming, so one August night we decided to drive our truck back to the woodshed and investigate the noises.

"While pulling up, we could hear very faint rustling in the dense tree line entering the state land, and so I started spotlighting the area when all of a sudden a large tree came crashing down, and as I homed in on the exact area, something absolutely roared at us with deeper octaves than anything I could have mustered up. Was around midnight, and our nearest neighbor is three-quarters of a mile down our gravel road. Absolutely scared the heck out of my wife and me. All the years of living in Upstate NY (Adirondack Mountains), I never ever experienced anything like that.

"After that night we started emptying the woodshed and took the structure down. Now it's a zone in the rear of our property that even our dogs won't go near. There are things out there that people have to see to believe. I couldn't care less what anyone thinks. We both know what we heard. Be safe out there, please."

SEPTEMBER 1997

In 2019 I was contacted by a lady who had a roadside sighting back in September 1997 of a large hairy creature on Route 86 at approximately 6:20 a.m. southbound early one morning on her way to work. Upon speaking to her over the phone, she appeared to be a levelheaded person and also had family and relatives from the Saranac Lake area community. She described the creature as a "big shaggy ape-looking thing" that swung its arms as it walked. The woman noticed the creature turned its head to look at the motorist as it walked across the road before disappearing into the woods. The area that she described in her sighting was forested on both sides of the road, suggesting that it may have been migrating through that vicinity, as she thought it may have been headed towards Lake Colby. She described the creature to be brown in color and taller than a man and was about 100–150 yards away from her as it crossed the road.

AUGUST 1996

"Myself and six friends were camping at Pine Pond in the lower Saranac Lake region. It was around dusk, and my friend and I were fishing in our canoe. The other members of our party were at camp preparing supper, and about a quarter mile away through the forest from our location in the canoe in the middle of the lake.

"My friend and I were speaking openly, not attempting to be quiet in any way. I was scanning the northern bank of the lake, which I knew quite well, when I noticed a strange shape on the edge of the wood line. It was about fifty yards away. Immediately I pointed it out to my friend, and he spotted it instantly. The shape was about three and a half feet off the ground at its highest point. At first we both thought it was a black bear standing broadside, but after a few seconds I realized that was not the case. We started to row towards it somewhat cautiously. Just as my friend whispered, 'It's a bear,' the thing stood up. It had been crouching there on its feet like a catcher from a baseball team.

"It was about seven feet tall and was very dark brown in color. Its face was hairy yet fleshy around the upper cheeks.

Its eyes were dark in color but clearly visible and had a brightness about them. Upon talking afterwards, we both agreed that we saw slight movement of its head and hands. It stood there for what seemed like ten seconds looking at us. It tilted its head slightly up as if it was sniffing the air. As if all this wasn't strange enough, we then heard snapping twigs about fifty feet behind it. The creature turned its torso to the left and looked to its side. It immediately turned back towards us and then spun 180 degrees around and darted into the wood line like a cat. We then heard the sound of movement for about ten more seconds; then we heard nothing. To this day, I have no idea what made the noise behind it.

"After staying put in the canoe for about ten minutes, my friend (against my wishes) decided to paddle to the spot on shore and investigate for tracks. There were only two discernible markings in the sand, which were obscured from the pivoting of its feet when it turned around. The whole experience was very, very upsetting. Although I can honestly say it did not attempt to threaten us in any way, it was scary as hell. That night I did not sleep one wink because I was so focused on every little noise that I heard. The next day we left. The other people in our party are convinced we saw a bear. It was no bear."

FEBRUARY 2005, CHAZY LAKE

"My family owns a home on Chazy Lake in the northeast corner of the Adirondacks. I spent many weekends there and often wake up early on Monday morning in order to get into work (about one hour away). In February of 2005, I had gotten up and left the house at about 6:30 a.m. Approximately two miles down the Chazy Lake Road, headed towards the town of Saranac, is where I had my sighting.

"A ditch approximately three feet wide and two feet deep

runs alongside the road. There was probably about a foot of snow on the ground. As I was driving, I saw something dark stand up from the inside of the ditch and head into the woods. When I saw it, it was probably 150–200 yards in front of me. It appeared to have a human shape but was slouched over. I could not tell the height, nor could I give an approximate weight. The sighting lasted probably no more than five seconds. I saw the upper two-thirds of its body, which appeared to be dark brown or black in color.

"I told my wife about it that night, and we joked about it for a bit, saying it must have been a Bigfoot. In all honesty, I thought I had either seen a bear, or my eyes were playing tricks on me. I hadn't thought about the sighting for quite some time until I read about a similar sighting in Clinton County."

SUMMER 2014, LAKE PLACID

"I recall my trip in a rowboat. I traveled in it all the way across Lake Placid to the other side, starting from the marina to the boat launch that connects with a trail that goes up to White Face Mountain. I camped in a spot near the boat launch. Late at night in my tent, I heard a scream off in the distance. I tried to reason what it was. I thought it might be kids, but I thought, 'Wait a second, kids being out there in the deep wilderness at night, making a scream-type howl?' My thought was unlikely to be what I heard, and it was loud. I also was thinking, 'Did I just hear my first Sasquatch scream?' I was thinking, 'Wow !' And saying, 'Wow!' And near the Price Chopper store in Lake Placid.

"A few years ago, I was camping in the same spot just about five minutes from Price Chopper down the road going towards Saranac Lake. I left my camp for a while. When I came back, I noticed my tent had been pushed down somewhat. I slowly approached my tent. I stopped and looked around. I peeled off my rain fly to my tent and saw the damage, to my amazement. Whatever it was had great strength to grab my high-density tent poles on top of my tent, through my rain fly, and snap the poles all the way through. I also noticed tree saplings uprooted near my camp. I thought that was odd. I still to this day have the poles from my tent. Just so when I tell the story to someone, they might believe me and not think I am making this up.

"Go with Jesus, people, because we are definitely living in the Last Days; strange and unusual oddities are happening around the world so quickly like never before has happened in the history of this world. God have mercy."

JULY 2014

"I was driving home through the mountains from a concert on Route 8 in Hamilton County at about 12:37 a.m. I hit a creature that was carrying a deer with my car. My car is damaged from the hood to the rear by this creature, and I know it is at the least injured and its DNA may be on my car. When I saw the creature that was carrying the deer, about to step into the roadway, I hit the brakes but was only able to slow down minimally before impact. I did not really believe in Bigfoot before last night, and I'm still shaken up and have not been able to share this story with anyone.

"The creature was huge, at least seven and a half feet tall. I've seen drawings and such of Bigfoot, and this creature looked similar, but had white around its hairline, and its fur was dark brown, almost black. I'm shaking as I'm writing this, and I'm in such disbelief that this happened to me. I can't even report this accident to the police, and I don't know what I will tell my insurance company."

Personal note: The witness claims the creature caused damage to her vehicle that included crushing her windshield wipers together, breaking pieces of the passenger side, and leaving smears of dirt and blood on the rear window. The witness wasn't able to observe how the creature reacted after her vehicle made impact with it, such as vocalizations or other audible sounds. However, auto accidents can temporarily leave a person stunned long enough for something to evade the witness. Due to the fact that the accident took place several years ago, recovering the vehicle for DNA samples would be next to impossible.

JULY 1998

The eyewitnesses describe their encounter on Chazy Lake Road off Route 374, near the Saranac Lake area, from Dannemora headed west towards Lyon Mountain. "My wife and I were on a Sunday drive on our Honda Goldwing motorcycle, heading south on the Chazy Lake Road towards Saranac, New York. We live in Cadyville, NY, which is about four miles east of Saranac. The Chazy Lake Road is a not-too-often-traveled road in a heavily wooded area.

"I was commenting to my wife how quiet our motorcycle was, and I pulled the clutch lever in to allow the motorcycle to coast. As we rounded the next curve, we both saw two large black hairy figures in the middle of the road, facing each other. They looked in our direction, then immediately ran into the woods. They both headed into the woods in opposite directions. They ran quite fast, slightly bent at the waist. When we arrived at the point where we saw them, there was no sign of them.

"When this happened, my wife said, 'Did you see what I think I just saw?' I said yes. We agreed we would not tell anyone of our experience for fear of ridicule. I would estimate their size to be at least six feet tall and at least two hundred plus pounds."

AUGUST 2010, CASCADE LAKE

"I spend most of the summers camping in and around the Adirondacks in my Dodge Caravan. This particular summer I had stopped at Cascade Lake to spend a few days camping. I had slept soundly the previous night and had woken up around 7:00 a.m. I decided to get up and start making my breakfast. I had just started the kettle on the camp stove when I looked over at upper Cascade Lake and could see the mist rising off the surface of the lake. I grabbed my iPhone and walked about fifty yards to the edge of the lake to get a picture.

"As I approached the breakwall, I noticed a dark brown object on the opposite side of the lake at the shore. At first I couldn't make out what it was, but it seemed to be sitting at the water's edge. I then realized that it must be a bear. The animal looked like it was doing something in the water with its paws, as I could hear a faint splashing sound.

"I thought it would be a good idea to get a picture, so I brought my iPhone up to face level and tried to focus on the animal. As I was focusing, the animal stood up on two legs. I was startled and pulled down my phone to see this with my own eyes. It took a step towards the treeline and stopped. Almost methodically, as it stopped, it turned its whole upper body to the left and stared at me for a couple of seconds. When it turned to stare at me, I could not make out any facial features, but I knew that it saw me. The upper body was massive and stocky like a football player's build. It had very long arms that went well below its waist. I could also make out what I assume were the shape of hands. It walked upright and paused before slowly turning its upper body to look directly at me. It stared at me for approximately five to ten seconds and turned back to face the treeline. It took one or two steps and disappeared into the forest.

"I immediately went cold and got scared. As I ran back to my campsite, my only thought was that it was going to go left or right. If it went right, it would have to go into the water, and if it went left, it was headed directly for my campsite. I decided that it was best to get the hell out of Dodge, so to speak.

"I arrived back at my campsite in under a minute. My dog was still asleep on the front seat and didn't stir at all. I opened the passenger-side sliding door of my van and started to throw all of the camping gear back into the van, making quite a mess inside as I did. I closed the door and then jumped into the driver's seat and floored the gas to leave. As I was driving out, I kept looking out my left driver's side window to see if I could observe it again, but I saw nothing. I drove all the way into Lake Placid and parked at a mall parking lot to gather my thoughts and think about what had taken place. I was pretty shaken up, as I kept replaying the experience over and over in my head, trying to make sense of what I had seen."

SUMMER 2012

An eyewitness was on his way home along County Route 37 at around 11:30 p.m. on June 20 when something got his attention. He described a fast-moving creature that crossed the road fifty feet from his car. "I was going sixty; it crossed the road from right to left in less than a second," he wrote. "It was not a deer. I've seen plenty of deer." After posting his story on social media, several other people came forward to describe similar experiences.

One of them had been plagued by several encounters with

a mysterious creature in the area for years. "The woods at the back of my house went on for miles," he wrote. "I was out there a couple nights, and I kept hearing a loud screaming noise. It sounded like nothing I ever heard before in my life. It sounded like a mix between an elephant and a bear. It goes right through you; it's deafening.

"The summer of 2013 was when it started getting really bad. Every night I would have company over, and every time we were outside, we would hear this thing screaming. One day I came home from work at 8 a.m., and my neighbors were all outside. While I was at work, one of them ran through my yard and destroyed my birdhouse. There were big footprints through my whole yard and hair stuck in my fence."

Personal note: There wasn't any mention of what came about with the hair found on his fence. It would've been the smoking gun for DNA samples to identify what was frequenting his property.

During one of my trips to the Adirondacks, I was contacted by a landowner who was walking a trail one summer back in 1994. She went on to describe during her hike along the trail, she spotted what she described to be a large human covered in hair paralleling her from a ridge. The eyewitness described the creature as walking with its knees slightly bent while walking on two feet, similar to a human. She said its hands hung down slightly below its knees when it walked. She estimated it to be at least eight feet in height with a very powerful build and massive shoulders. Due to the distance between her and the creature, she was not able to give any facial features other than it had a dark brown color to it.

Based on my observation, most hikers don't camp on a ridge. Ridges generally have more wind, more inclement weather, and usually don't have shelter or water for campers.

I've theorized many times that if researchers camped out on ridges and looked for wildlife paths and stayed in groups no smaller than three, more Bigfoot encounters would occur and more information would be discovered. I find this eyewitness's story to be very credible.

Over the years during my research, I've been connecting the dots and understanding winter and summer movement and habits of these hominids. In my area of Vermont, there are trappers with long lines, and many private landowners. We do on occasion hear about folks finding tracks here in the winter. I have had people tell me, "They go to remote areas in winter." Fine, so do trappers and small aircraft. You can tell a moose track from a bear track at one thousand feet above ground level in an airplane.

We do have reports here in the summer, admittedly they are few and far between, but there are some. I find no evidence to support the hibernation theory at all. I have heard the theory that bears hibernate so why can't Bigfoot? Bigfoot is not a bear, for starters. There are a lot of changes that happen within a bear's body metabolically to make hibernation possible; the metabolic rate with a human hominid would differ significantly from a typical bear. While these hominids are typically depicted as a shy creature that has no interest in interacting with humans, throughout history, there have been numerous incidents of Bigfoot attacks.

In the summer of 2021, my trip to Saranac Lake was to interview a local artist in regard to his encounter. As he was making his way out to Tupper Lake to stay at his uncle's cabin for the weekend, he noticed some trees that appeared to be broken and thrown onto the dirt driveway leading to the cabin. He explained that he never had any direct sightings with a Sasquatch but had seen large, five-toed, human-looking footprints on the property. In the back of the cabin, they had a fifty-five-gallon barrel trash can that they used for unwanted food scraps. He explained that they had heard a noise in the middle of the night, but never got up to check, figuring it was a bear. The next morning they went out and found that the garbage can was gone. Nothing was dumped on the ground, and all the contents along with the barrel were gone. They searched the property and found nothing.

WHITEHALL

Located at the southern end of Lake Champlain, in the Adirondack foothills, Whitehall has been called the Bigfoot capital of the East Coast. It's also named the birthplace of the United States Navy, and it served as the backdrop for Revolutionary War activity under the command of Benedict Arnold. For a small town with just over four thousand people, this area carries a lot of historical value. Stories of rocks being tossed at hikers, loud screams that pierce the air, and even sightings of something unknown have filled locals' lives for generations.

Every culture has stories about things that go bump in the night. Myths, legends and yarns spun around a campfire to entertain, to caution, and sometimes to scare the listener. Some of these same stories are shared across the globe, perhaps rooted in events that took place a long time ago, or in creatures that lurk in the dark places of the world but are rarely seen. Its dark woods, looming mountains, and long winters have conjured up stories of creatures and monsters for its inhabitants for thousands of years.

To the Abenaki people, an Algonquin tribe from the area, the idea of a Sasquatch isn't foreign at all. Winter stories tell of encounters with the Kiwak, a looming figure over eight feet tall, covered in dark hair, with red glowing eyes and ear-piercing screams. Their scream is so piercing it can stop the hearts of its victims. Stories of these monsters aren't relegated to just one tribe, though. Some Native American tribes refer to the same creature, such as the Wendigo of the Anishinabe.

JANUARY 5, 2020

Daytime sighting. At approximately noon of January 5, a local woman observed a large dark-brown-colored hairy creature walking towards the wood line just off Stalker Road. The witness said, in her own words, "It had beautiful auburn hair that glistened in the sun." The next day, she and a local investigator visited the area, but no evidence was found.

SUMMER 2018

A man who was on his way to Vermont claims to have seen the legendary creature approximately half a mile away from where a similar-looking creature was spotted in 2006, according to a *New York Post* report. The motorist claimed to have witnessed a seven-foot-tall creature hopping over a guardrail on Route 4 in Whitehall. The eyewitness declined to be named because of possible ridicule, though he did observe that the creature was hairy, had two legs, wide shoulders, and a small neck.

In my observation of eyewitness reports in Whitehall, I found that August, September and October are popular months for this activity, indicating a migration route through Whitehall and into Vermont. But there's a real consistency with the reports. Roadside sightings while driving at night, and seeing a large hairy creature crossing in front of a passing motorist are the most common scenarios. A forest road is the most likely place for a person to have the opportunity to see the creature. Unfortunately, the driver did not take a picture of the hominid, as the event happened too quickly.

JUNE 2019

At approximately 5 p.m., an eyewitness was walking his dog along Main Street in Whitehall. A nearby tractor-trailer truck was rounding the corner when the witness observed a hairy creature standing up. He then turned away, walking quickly, and glanced over his shoulder as he watched the creature smoothly walking away. Surprisingly, the dog didn't notice the creature as they walked away, but he stated that it "moved in a fluid motion." Other locals found twelve-inch footprints and a bedding area nearby.

According to the evidence left behind, that creature was estimated to be approximately six plus feet in height, two hundred pounds or more, with a two-foot stride, with a slender appearance. The witness described the head as having a pointed cone shape and no definitive forehead and no visible neck. Broad shoulders about three feet wide. Long arms past the knees, no mention of gender, and no noticeable odor. Face was not visible but had a dark brown color to the body. The creature was seen headed west towards a forested area near the East Bay.

JANUARY 1981

An eyewitness describes his encounter in the East Bay area and gives a Google Earth location of 43 degrees 34' 13.94" north, 73 degrees 23' 34.67" west. "Late one night a girlfriend and I drove out to the East Bay and stopped to talk for a while. After a few moments spent parked near the bridge, I saw what looked to be a man walking across the marshy area to our left. The distance, I'm assuming, was about two hundred to three hundred yards. This I gauged by seeing a fence line in the distance. We both watched as this man approached the fence line. He cleared it without stopping, simply stepping over it as if it were a low stool. Knowing that the snow was not that deep or that hard to support a man of his size, and that it was highly unlikely for anyone to be out on the marshes at that time of night, I stepped out of the car to get a better look.

"As soon as I had gotten out of the car, the man changed course and began heading straight towards us. I closed the car door to cancel the interior light and prevent showing my location. At this point, the man broke into a run. His speed was incredible. He closed the distance between us very quickly. My girlfriend was screaming for me to get back into the car at this point. I got back into my car, and she drove back over the bridge into NY. As we went, I looked behind us and saw that we were being pursued, although we were building a gap. As soon as we returned to hardtop road, he broke off pursuit and ran back into the forest near the bridge. We returned to town and never spoke of this incident to anyone other than two trusted friends.

"I have since told friends and relatives that I saw 'something' out there but could not say that it was any animal I had ever seen, nor could it have been any man. I should add at this time I had spent sixteen years working and playing outdoors. I had encountered all of the major predators of our area, knew their habits and habitats. I know I did not mistake an animal for a humanoid creature that night. I will further add that I am now a natural resource scientist with fifteen years of experience studying and reporting information based on my observation and analysis. I still can't state with precision what it is I saw that night."

Personal note: I have visited that location on numerous occasions, and I'm very familiar with the fence line that he spoke of. His observation of it clearing the fence without breaking stride would in reality need a body height of at least eight feet or taller. The eyewitness also observed that the creature's motions were animal-like and not humanlike, and noted that its arms were swinging as it moved. It should also be noted that the witness described the creature's movement as a cross-country skier when it approached him in his car. Us humans tend to have that bobbing-of-the-head movement when we walk, giving a clear indication that their skeletal structures are anatomically designed slightly differently from humans'.

JANUARY 1989

A property owner near the Vermont state line discovered a set of large human footprints that were estimated to be almost twenty inches in length, near some broken tree branches, while walking in the woods. The witnesses stated that the tree branches were about fifteen feet off the ground and appeared to be out of the ordinary. The two men both had the feeling of being watched, and due to the fact that the sun was setting, they decided to head back home. During their walk back home, they both felt as if they were being followed, but didn't see any sign of anyone else with them in the woods. The next day, the witness stated the following.

"Then the next morning I awoke (6:30 a.m.) to see a large creature about twenty feet from the house. (I slept on the fold-out couch, and the entire front of the house has windows.) It must have been at least ten feet tall, as the windows are fifteen feet off the ground, and it was no more than five feet below me. It wandered around for a while, and I did not dare move. It was brown and looked very human except for its size and forehead and obviously the hair.

"After about five minutes, it walked towards the house and up a bank. As it passed the house, it banged on the wall, and I thought its arm would come right through. My friend was wakened by this and came in, and I told him what I had seen. We both decided not to go back out to follow the tracks."

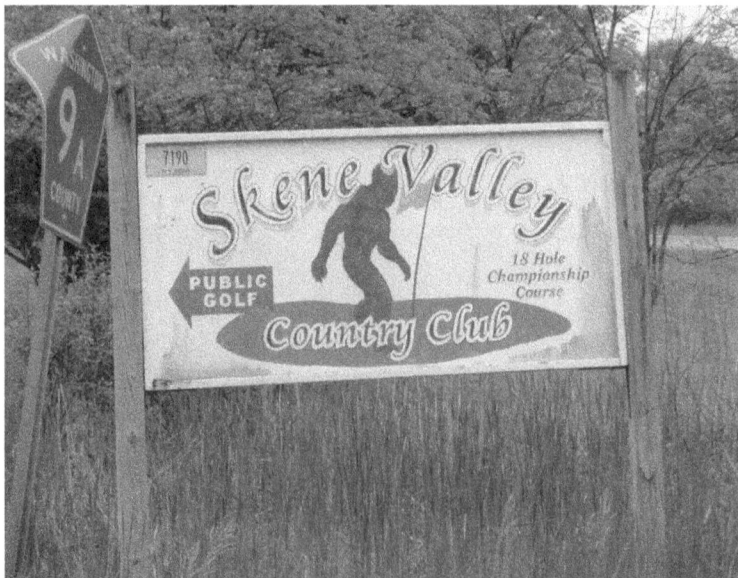

MAY 1975

At approximately 11:30 p.m., Skene Valley Country Club owner Cliff Sparks encountered a large two-legged hairy "sloth-like" creature while watering the first green of his golf course. Its head had virtually no neck, with a cone-shaped cranium, and it walked in an awkward manner. "It lumbered and walked with a very clumsy gait. The creature had a different leg and knee action than a man. I don't know how, just different." Sparks was mesmerized by the eyes of the creature, as they were red glowing, non-reflective. He also noted that it stared at his dog, which became uncharacteristically subdued. He observed it quietly and then saw it quickly crashing through the woods.

Then two boys had a sighting to become part of the continuum of the region's hairy-biped sightings. "I think more people believe now," says Sparks, who, after the sighting, decided to add Bigfoot's image (hoisting a golf flag) to his club's logo. "I think some people probably think I'm crazy, but they weren't there. They didn't see it. And since then, other golfers have gotten glimpses of the creature.

Personal note: I personally met Mr. Sparks back in 2010, and I have visited the location where his sighting took place, and I found him to be a very honest and credible witness. Clifford N. Sparks, seventy-six, owner of Skene Valley Country Club, passed away September 9, 2012, at home with his family by his side after a long battle with lung disease.

AUGUST 1976

The details of the Gosselin interactions with Bigfoot are compelling, and they have been discussed often in literature.

On August 24, 1976, Paul Gosselin, who at the time was eighteen years old, was out driving around with two friends,

Marty Paddock and Bart Kinney. (Kinney is rarely mentioned.) The three were driving down Abair Road, in the Town of Hampton, near Whitehall, New York, when they heard a female screaming. They all initially saw the creature near the Abair Road telephone pole. Gosselin and Paddock glanced out into the vast field to see what the noise was coming from. The two reported seeing a large, apelike creature, between seven feet and eight feet tall, darting toward their car. Immediately, they both got in the car and stormed into the Village of Whitehall to report what they saw to police.

Gosselin's brother, Brian, was the on-duty police officer in the Village of Whitehall that night when his father, brother, and Paddock came flying back into the village. "They were so strung out with excitement and fear," he said. The following night was Gosselin's night off from work, so he decided to go out and see for himself.

Gosselin was down in the meadows, where his father and brother had seen the creature, while a state trooper was up at the top of the hill on Abair Road. The two were communicating via radio. After about an hour and a half, Gosselin was radioed by the state trooper, who said, "Brian, what the #%*!@#% is that? I'm heading out of here." The trooper sped away, leaving Gosselin alone.

He said he continued to hear noises, "not twigs snapping, limbs snapping," and something suddenly made him decide to turn his spotlight in the direction of the sound. "I turned my spotlight on it, and it was now about thirty to thirty-five feet away," Gosselin recalled. "It was over seven feet tall, probably around four hundred pounds. When I put the spotlight on it, it raised its hands – they weren't paws, they were hands; I could see the fingers – to cover its eyes. They were red and about the diameter of a mayonnaise cover; they didn't glow like a deer's eyes in headlights, though."

Gosselin said at that moment he had a million different thoughts run through his head, when suddenly the creature turned and retreated, making a lengthy guttural noise. "It's impossible for a human to make that noise," he said. "This thing showed no aggression though. If it wanted me, it could have had me, let's put it that way."

Gosselin sat in the field for about fifteen more minutes, trying to figure out what he had just encountered. "I knew everything it wasn't; it wasn't a man, it wasn't a bear, it wasn't an ape," he said. Since that moment, Gosselin has been 100 percent a believer. "The New York-Vermont border area has had several underreported instances." Abair Road sort of made Whitehall famous for it.

Our condolences to Paul Gosselin's family and friends. He leaves many people behind. He was born August 25, 1957, in Glens Falls, New York, to the late Wilfred and Pauline Gosselin. Paul graduated from Whitehall High School and joined the Army National Guard. As his local *Post-Star* obituary noted, Paul was a roofer by trade. He loved the outdoors, whether he was mowing the lawn, planting his garden, or building bird houses. He was also good at carving walking sticks and building picnic tables. He was a hunter and an avid fisherman; he and Rhonda would spend hours on Lake Champlain fishing. He also enjoyed riding his motorcycle. Paul met and married his wife, Rhonda, in July 2011. Paul was predeceased by his parents, Wilfred and Pauline Gosselin; his sister, Gale; and brothers, David and Bruce.

4 REPORTS IN 2006

On August 18, a man was driving toward South Bay at about 6:45 p.m., near the waste treatment plant, when he spotted a large creature, all black, standing near the fence line. The creature was described as being over seven feet tall with "big wide shoulders and a big bull neck." The witness claimed the creature was reaching for something at a forty-five-degree angle.

September 4. At approximately 8:45 p.m., a mysterious figure is spotted by four people driving on Route 4. It was standing on the side of the road. "It had a white face and black hair and was about seven feet tall," the witnesses observed.

Late October. A seven-foot-tall humanlike creature is spotted by three teenage girls while lake camping in East Whitehall. One of the girls said, "We all saw it at the same time, and we all screamed." She says that she froze while her companions ran off.

On September 3, a man was traveling through Whitehall with his family on Route 4 when they spotted a six-to-seven-foot-tall brown hairy hominid standing near the road less than one mile before reaching the village of Whitehall. Very little detail was given on the description of the creature spotted, i.e., facial features, gestures, direction of travel. These, along with numerous other eyewitness reports, are a clear indication of a migration route used as passage from the Adirondacks and into Vermont, and Whitehall serves as a midway point.

Personal note: There have been many documented cases where Sasquatch makes its presence known to kids in what appears to be an attempt at interaction. From numerous documentations that Bigfoot knows that kids pose no threat, but attempts to act non-aggressive and invite the interaction fails time after time. The sheer size of the creature would be enough to scare the kids into Jesus. And the reaction that the creature saw from the kids probably let the creature know that they were frightened, and it wasn't welcome on their property. Which could be the reason it didn't return.

"This might sound crazy to most of you, but my husband and myself have had some strange things take place on our property in the past several years. Sometimes our trash bags would go missing when left outside; other times we found tree branches thrown in our backyard. And sometimes in the summer we would hear strange yells or howls late at night. Most didn't go out seeking sightings of anything, yet we're all seeing the same thing throughout the US.

"They're noticeably in my area (Upstate NY, Appalachian Mountains vicinity) during the summer months. Other than my first time venturing out and unintentionally ending up in their stomping grounds, now I know exactly where to look. And sure enough, summer after summer, they're in the area. Winter, I go out, and they're nowhere to be seen or heard. HOWEVER, this is nothing to play around with by any means. Have to always be able to get away quickly if necessary."

The Big Apple Diner located on RT.4 in Whitehall, NY. They have a fair amount of parking and an easy to find location. The staff is very pleasant, efficient and friendly

Route 4 entering into Whitehall

DOGMAN

As any Bigfoot researcher will tell you, the deeper you dive into Bigfoot cases, the stranger things get. And as time went on, I couldn't ignore the reports of these unexplained case reports of upright walking K-9s, or "Dogmen," as most of us like to call them. Most of the people who tell their tales of shock and wonder at meeting a wolf that walks upright still appear reluctant to talk, while others simply wish to confess their experience to someone who won't tell them they are crazy. No matter how weird their story is, I've heard stranger tales before.

Dogmen have been encountered and sighted all over North America and around the globe. Although they look like the werewolves of lore in movies, they are not werewolves. They are believed to be a species with both human and K-9 attributes. Because of the similarities between the species of *Homo sapiens* (humans) and Canidae (wolves/dogs), they will also be referred to as *Homo canidae*.

Dogmen have been reported by eyewitnesses to be very muscular and as tall as ten feet in height when standing bipedally. They have a humanlike form from the shoulders down to the knees. They do not have front paws, but instead have elongated hands like humans but with long fingers. There are sharp claws on the fingertips. They can walk and run on all fours as well as bipedally. In fact, many eyewitness reports state that when a Dogman goes from standing on all fours to standing on two legs, or vice versa, a loud popping sound is heard from the joints. The sound is thought to be the joints of the creature acclimating to each mode for walking and running.

In my years of research, I've heard many stories about upright canines before, and it's likely that you may have heard another similar legend about "the Beast of Bray Road." The descriptions of that creature in the town of Elkhorn, Wisconsin, are nearly identical. It fits in perfectly with all the werewolf tales that have been present in human culture for centuries. If a creature is hiding in northern lower Wisconsin, that would be a good area. Much of the county is covered by national forest. However, the sightings are scattered all over the state and in Michigan, including the Upper Peninsula. However, the majority seem to be centered in the northwest part of the Lower Peninsula, especially around the greater Traverse City area.

The legend of the Dogman has many true believers, and not just in Michigan. Reporter Linda S. Godfrey, who was the first to document the legend of the Beast of Bray Road, wrote a book documenting the creature too. In the book, she notes she receives letters and emails from coast to coast, from the north woods of Maine to the coasts of California, from people claiming to have seen a canine-like animal with human characteristics. Having interviewed many of the eyewitnesses, she says many are hesitant to share the experience with others.

Many of the tales are quick encounters on lonely roads while an eyewitness is driving. They catch a brief glimpse of a doglike creature in the headlights either crossing the road or standing on the shoulder before it vanishes from sight. Some even detail alleged attacks by the beast. Many of them are told by hunters or campers who had unexpected run-ins with the creature in a remote section of forest. Some even claim the beast left claw and bite marks on homes or property before vanishing.

One interesting detail of many of the sightings is that eyewitnesses claim the creature can switch between walking on two feet and four feet quite easily. One of the common denominators that remains consistent is the distinct sound of bones popping or knuckles cracking when these creatures begin to stand upright. Perhaps this is the shifting of the joints, or the adaptations of its skeletal structure.

Wisconsin and Michigan seem to be the epicenter for a being that is a derivative of the English "werewolf." As the French settled the new world, rougarou became the typical name for the monster in the Louisiana bayou, these wolflike K-9s. Texas has also had its fair share of Dogman sightings. Travel deep within the boggy terrain of the Louisiana bayous to discover a legendary supernatural creature. For those who haven't heard, I'm talking about the rougarou. Tales of this mysterious creature are especially popular during the spooky Halloween season. Tales of this swamp legend are connected to Francophone cultures. The rougarou itself is actually the Acadian variation of the name. The French are believed to have originally called it the loup-garou, loup being the French word for "wolf" and garou for "man".

Most sightings of Dogmen take place in rural places, large parks, and wooded areas. They are often spotted high up in trees and are said to move very quickly for a species of its size and weight. Sightings have also taken place near cities and highly populated areas. Dogmen have been reported as often peeking through the windows of homes. They also tap on the window's glass with their finger-claws. One report describes a Dogman playing "peekaboo" with a very little girl from outside her bedroom window before her father walked in, and the Dogman ran off. They often rattle and turn the knobs and handles of doors to houses. This behavior tends to happen at night.

Although many eyewitnesses have encountered *Homo canidae* and escaped unharmed, others have reported that they can be dangerous and sometimes kill humans. One eyewitness states that he believes that there are good ones and bad ones, just like human beings. He also believes they congregate in tribes, not packs. It is advised that if one does encounter a Dogman to proceed with caution because they can be deadly. These cryptids appear to be highly intelligent and have been noted to know what guns are. They tend to avoid firearms, so warning shots fired at the sky from a gun or rifle may cause one to flee.

Dr. Melba S. Ketchum, DVM, the director of DNA Diagnostics Inc., has done DNA testing on Sasquatch hair and found that the mitochondrial DNA, the DNA passed down from mother to child, is from a human woman. She states:

> "The genome sequencing shows that Sasquatch [mitochondrial DNA] is identical to modern *Homo sapiens*, but Sasquatch [nuclear DNA] is a novel, unknown hominin related to *Homo sapiens* and other primate species. Our data indicate that the North American Sasquatch is a hybrid species, the result of males of an unknown hominin species crossing with female *Homo sapiens*."

Sasquatch and Dogmen fit the Nephilim profile, and Dr. Ketchum's DNA study corroborates the theory. More on her study. How an angelic/spiritual being may transform into a physical being with working genetics is unknown. However, the Nephilim theory may also explain the legends of Minotaurs, centaurs, mermaids and other animal hybrids in history.

From time to time, I will hear about a weird hybrid beast some call a "snout-nosed" Bigfoot. It sounds like a cross between Dogman and a man ape, which is not genetically feasible. A few writers have defended that concept by saying that baboons have facial features, snouts, fangs and visible ears that resemble those of K-9s. The trouble with this notion is that Bigfoot is very much a member of the human scale. Another observation is that baboons don't really fit most sighting reports of Bigfoot or a manwolf. A baboon's body will max out at about forty inches in height, so they would never fit the reports of a six-to-seven-foot-tall hairy hominid. Yet there hasn't been a single baboon captured in North America live or dead in history. Others have often theorized that these manwolf reports are misidentified bears or other animals.

Although I have used the term Dogman and manwolf interchangeably in this chapter, since no one has any definitive answer as to what these cryptid K-9s really are, the idea of Dogman has deep roots in human culture and religion. And some behavioral traits of Dogman are different that those of a traditional werewolf.

Native Americans, Indians, teach their kids different skills. Aside from hunting, tracking, respect for the animals and forest, etc. One of the Natives whom I knew said his tribal elders warned him of what was out there. I asked another Native if they were real; he looked at me for about ten seconds before answering, just gave me that weird look. He said yeah, they were on the reservation lands. He would leave them the internal organs as a gift after the hunt. The really weird thing he told me was he would give most others the chills. Some sounded a bit crazy or weird to me. His father told him to do that to have a successful hunt, and to not be bothered, leave them part of the kill. He said they are on Indian reservation land as well. You have to be part of that tribe to hunt there or be personally invited by a member of the tribe to hunt with them. They said they know where they hang out and avoid their dens or areas.

Some Alaskan tribes don't go into certain areas because their cryptids are aggressive if you get too close. It's like an uneasy truce, they leave them alone, and the cryptids leave the Indians alone. If a tribe loses kids or their women, the whole tribe of able-bodied males will track it down and kill it. Pretty much tribal hunters and trackers can track anything down, especially if they are motivated. Their Indian law enforcement, or sheriffs, won't say anything. What happens on the reservation stays on the reservation, especially if it concerns their people. Cryptids are known to pick up their dead and wounded, might give you a small break if you can injure one or if you kill enough. Force them to regroup. Either will run away if you get the alpha, or come back at you again but a whole lot more cautiously. If they are tracking you and you can't outrun them, pick your spot to fight and ambush them. It's a game of chess and attrition. If they know where you live or where your car is at, they might just wait for you there. Don't underestimate them and think they are stupid.

Anubis, the Egyptian god, could have been inspired by Dogmen.

Although I have used the terms "Dogman" and "wolfman" almost interchangeably, since no one really knows for sure what these K-9 cryptids are, the idea of Dogman has deep roots in human culture and religion. Some of the traits of Dogmen are often quite different than those of the traditional werewolf. And because dogs are so close to humans socially, Dogmen have historically been conceived of as odd humans with K-9 heads.

In addition to the Hopi and Navajo tribes, I've discussed the Native American phenomenon of Skinwalkers in my previous book. Skinwalkers are entities created by magic rituals that look like animals but are spirit doubles of the shaman that come from the physical body. However, I don't think that this is what eyewitnesses are experiencing in Upstate New York.

I'm often asked if these unknown K-9s might really be unknown apes. The questioner usually means Bigfoot, but apes have been brought up in question. Bigfoot walks upright and has a manlike skeletal structure, and they are flat footed. No pointed ears on top of the head, no long muzzle, no tail, and don't walk on clawed toe pads. In both cases, K-9s' and primates' physical structure and movements are so different that witnesses who have a good look at a Dogman or Bigfoot are usually pretty sure of what they saw.

The *Oxford English Dictionary* defines the word cryptid as "An animal whose existence or survival is disputed or unsubstantiated, such as the yeti." For the following witnesses to living cryptids, there is no dispute. In this series of National Cryptid Society's case files, you will read what the witnesses have experienced in their own words. Keep an open mind when reading these accounts, and also remember one's perception and memory of an event can be influenced by the emotions felt at the time of the occurrence. The contributors to this series of articles are doing the best they can to recount what are in some cases very shocking and traumatic experiences. Remember, these accounts, as told by witnesses, are not being presented as evidence of any event. Rather, they are the recollection from memory from everyday, ordinary people who want to be heard.

Italian Historian, Marco Polo -1271-95 AD:

"Angamanain is a very large Island. The people are without a king and are Idolaters, and no better than wild beasts. And I assure you all the men of this Island of Angamanain have heads like dogs, and teeth and eyes likewise; in fact, in the face they are all just like big mastiff dogs! They have a quantity of spices; but they are a most cruel generation, and eat everybody that they can catch, if not of their own race. They live on flesh and rice and milk, and have fruits different from any of ours."

The Travels of Marco Polo, Book 3, chapter 13
Greek Doctor, Ctesias of Cnidus - late 4th century BC:

"On these mountains there live men with the head of a dog, whose clothing is the skin of wild beasts. They speak no language, but bark like dogs, and in this manner make themselves understood by each other. Their teeth are larger than those of dogs, their nails like those of these animals, but longer and rounder. They inhabit the mountains as far as the river Indus. Their complexion is swarthy. They are extremely just, like the rest of the Indians with whom they associate. They understand the Indian language but are unable to converse, only barking or making signs with their hands and fingers by way of reply, like the deaf and dumb. They are called by the Indians Calystrii, in Greek Cynocephali. They live on raw meat. They number about 120,000.

Indica, chapter 72, St Isadore of Seville - around 636 AD:

"The Cynocephali are so-called because they have dogs' heads and their very barking betrays them as beasts rather than men." - *On Human Monstrosities, Etymologies Section*

There are four main different types or variants of these Dogman K-9s, and some may be subspecies or offshoots of other variants. People put them in different orders, considering there is no right or wrong order to put them in until we have an actual body to study.

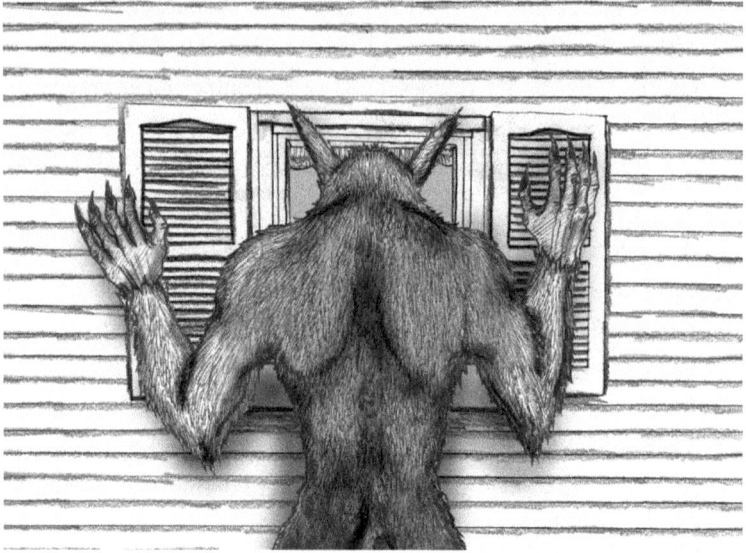

Cryptid K-9s have been known to be seen peeking through the windows of unsuspected victims. (Drawing courtesy of North American Dogman Project.)

TYPE 1 K9 VARIANT

The K-9-type Dogmen are described to have the head of a wolf or dog, and the upper torso has the physique of a human. The arms are long, and the elongated hands have claws. The thighs are humanlike, but the lower legs are reversed like those of a K-9, giving it the appearance that its legs are on backwards. The feet are large with claws and resemble those of a wolf. They come in a variety of colors but mostly black and are often said to have a thick tail. The various types of K-9s look like this to a degree but can vary in many ways. Some are described as having oversized heads. This one has been seen traveling in groups of three or four and sometimes solo. This type is also a very aggressive K-9 and is known to chase and terrorize people and sometimes destroy personal property such as fences, cabins, automobiles, etc.

TYPE 2 K9 VARIANT

Type 2 Dogmen are said to be similar to the K-9 type 1 but have a head like a hyena, and the upper torso has the physique of a human. The arms are long, and the elongated hands have claws. The thighs are also humanlike, but the lower legs are reversed like those of a type 1. The feet are large with claws and resemble those of a wolf. They come in a variety of colors but mostly brown and are often said to have a tail. The various types of K-9s look like this to a degree but can vary in many ways. Type 2s are also described as having oversized heads.

TYPE 3 K9 VARIANT

The Type 3 Dogman is described as having the upper torso and legs like a human but with very long arms. The face resembles that of a wolf or dog, but the muzzle tends to be shorter and not as pronounced. The snout, at times, can resemble the snout of a baboon. They are said not to have a tail. Type 3 Dogmen can come in a variety of colors and are often confused with Sasquatch or an ape because of their body style. However, this is not the case. Type 3 Dogmen have claws on their hands and feet, while Sasquatches, apes, and humans have fingernails. Type 3 Dogmen are not as often seen by eyewitnesses as the K-9 types are.

TYPE 4 K9 VARIANT

Similar to the type 1, it has an extremely large wolflike head and a soldier-type body, having the upper torso and legs like a human but with very long arms. The feet are large with claws and resemble those of a wolf. Often black in color, no reported tail. This type 4 is not reported in the Adirondacks to my knowledge; however, I could be wrong. Other researchers have claimed that there are seven or more variant Dogman types. I have listed the four main types; 1,2, and 3 are the most commonly reported among eyewitnesses in North America and Canada. These animals are highly intelligent and very dangerous, and extreme caution should be taken if encountering one.

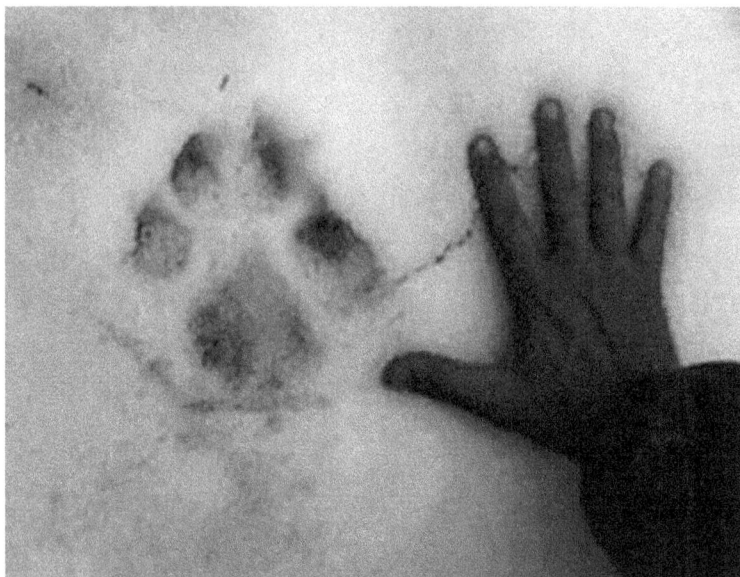

Photo courtesy of Dogmancryptid.com

Photo courtesy of North American Dogman Project

Photo courtesy of North American Dogman Project.

10 FEET

Human   Dogman

8 FEET

6 FEET

Drawing courtesy of Dogmancryptid.com

EYEWITNESS REPORTS

NORTH CREEK, 2022

"I just wanted to let you know that I think I may have recently (within the last month or so) seen a type 1 Dogman. I was driving along going to a doctor's appointment on a back highway, Route 28, in North Creek about twenty to twenty-five miles from my house. I am nearly deaf, so I am always watching the woods in case of deer or some kind of fowl coming out in front of my vehicle, and I tend to scan the wood lines a lot as I drive. On my right was a wood line relatively close to the road ... probably one hundred feet or so back from the street. It went on for probably one hundred yards and then receded straight back to about maybe one-sixteenth of a mile (probably between five hundred to one thousand feet?) and that's where I saw this totally jet-black wolf standing. But it was really strange looking.

"We have some farms around this area where they raise alpacas and even some white-tailed deer, and this animal's back was every bit as high as one of those! It had VERY long legs, extremely dark black fur, a thick chest and thin torso, and long pointed ears with tufts at the top. As I passed it and saw it, it saw me and watched me and turned its head as I drove past. I only saw it for maybe five seconds, but it was definitely a wolf-looking dog-type animal. But I've never seen a wolf with that long of legs before! If you've ever seen the world's biggest Great Dane, then you have an idea of how long this animal's legs were. Not quite that long but pretty close. I think it had a long bushy tail too, but I can't recall for sure. It was just too far away to see all the details, but it was really fascinating.

"We have several nests of bald eagles in this area, and the

last time I drove that highway, there was one eating some dead critter in the middle of the road and so that was really what I was looking for when I encountered this thing. Very interesting and freaky to see it, believe me. That's about all I saw, but I have never seen a wolf that black or with legs that long. I will have to research dogs a bit better to be sure, but I AM very familiar with dog breeds because that's what my wife and I do: we raise German shepherds, so I pretty much know my canines. Well, I just wanted to share that little story with you here. I have been reading and watching tons of videos on the subject and Sasquatch for a few years now. I find it fascinating. Weird but fascinating."

HUDSON RIVER TRAIL, MARCH 2020

"Late March 2020 after everyone was laid off, I saw a very large black wolf near the Hudson River Trail. It was about 6:30 a.m., and I was on my bicycle. I rode this trail every morning at the same time and saw the same people. I go out when the sun comes up.

"On this day I remember that not many people were out. In fact, I remember seeing almost no one. I was between North Shore Road and Hadley Mountain Trail Head. When I saw this animal, the trail was about ten feet wide there. The large black wolf looked over at me just as a wolf would and stared at me, then turned and went up the trail. It only took about four strides to clear the trail. It was larger than me, about six to seven feet in length. It was very low to the ground and massive. Its tail was as thick as a tennis ball and solid black. I am six feet tall and about two hundred pounds. My immediate reaction was 'I am never going to see this again,' and I was not scared. I was more fascinated by what I was seeing.

"I stopped pedaling but did not hit my brakes. About two

seconds later I reached the spot where I saw this creature, and it was completely gone. I looked up in the trees, down at the ground, and straight where it was headed, but it had completely disappeared. I could not see it, smell it, or hear it. Right off of the trail where it was headed, so it wasn't there either. It appeared to be a black wolf. After researching this, I found out that black wolves are not native to this area, but have not been seen since the late 1800s. It was an amazing discovery that I will never forget."

STONY CREEK, AUGUST 2014

"This takes place in the town of Stony Creek, NY. It's on the west side of Lake George, and there have been some weird things that have gone on there. I myself have had a weird experience while camping with my dad. It was the middle of the night, and we had just decided to go to sleep, and we went to our tent. It was about 1 a.m., and I was still up when I heard heavy footsteps, and I saw the shadow on the side of the tent while having only the moonlight, and it sniffed our tent and circled our tent for about five to ten minutes. The shadow looked about the size of a bear but much skinnier and very lanky. It eventually left, and in the morning me and my dad found the prints, which were the size of a bear's but looked like a dog's print. I haven't been back to that camping ground since."

STONY CREEK, JUNE 2006

"My daughter and I encountered something one night late in the town of Stoney Creek. It was at least seven feet tall or more, gray fur, and its eyes reflected yellow in the headlights (not the so-called red). We assumed maybe it was a Bigfoot.

We go up in the forest a lot to track coyote and have heard a lot of strange things, but that's the first time we saw the seven-foot-tall animal. It was standing on two legs too. We do have bears here, of course; however, they are black not gray. It stood there looking at us while we looked at it; then it just ran off on two legs. It was the most fantastic sighting. Not a human for sure. Definitely an animal. Besides, human eyes do not reflect in headlights, as most of you know. These eyes reflected a yellowish color."

TUPPER LAKE, OCTOBER 2012

"I saw something like a big black wolf just outside of Tupper Lake one night. I still can't explain it. I was driving down a rural road late at night and came to a curve where you had to slow down. On the left in front of a farm gate, I saw something in the corner of my eye that defied explanation. It looked to be a tall upright figure, with a wolf's head and upright ears with a long snout and covered in fur and standing on two legs, not moving, just sort of standing there as if my car's headlights made it pause. It really, really scared me, and I had this sense that I was seeing something that was like nothing I'd ever seen, and definitely no bear or ordinary wolf. There are bears and wolves in this part of New York. To this day I can't explain it, but I really believe it was maybe a Dogman."

JAY, VERMONT, 2018

"I live in a ridiculously small town in Vermont called Jay, right along the Canadian border. Aside from the town having very few businesses, we're also overshadowed by Jay State Park and Jay Peak. We're in the middle of nowhere. It was Christmas

Day, and it was just me and my single mom. I'm not a child anymore, a teenager, but I'm also not excited about Christmas to come. We knew the year would be quiet, so we just lined up a few movies to watch and made two steaks for dinner.

"As part of Vermont, it wasn't uncommon to see a deer or a moose come past our house. The town was quieter than usual because of the holiday, and this brought down more bears and raccoons than usual, looking for food in the cold Vermont winter. Hearing the bashing of trash cans was part of everyday life here. And this Christmas was no different. I Facetimed with my sister in New York. The day was fairly ordinary. I was looking forward to my mom going to sleep so I could play video games and not feel like I was ignoring her. The PlayStation was in the living room, which overlooked the road in front of the house. on the opposite side of the road was the forest. The television was in the corner next to the window, so it was hard not to see movement outside.

"Around 11 p.m. after my mom had been asleep for a while, I heard the trash cans banging again in the front of the house. I had taken the trash out earlier, and the dinner scraps were in there. I figured it was a raccoon trying to get what was left and bring it back to its family. But as I tried to ignore the noise, it got louder. Like something was digging at the bottom of the can. Out of the corner of my eye, I noticed movement, and I could tell it wasn't a raccoon or a bear. I thought I should take a closer look so I could make sure that whatever it was wasn't hurting anything. Chances were good that it would run away if I scared it. It wouldn't get aggressive or come to the house.

"I told my friends I was playing with that I needed to step away because something was getting into our trash. We were playing virtually, and they all laughed because none of them lived anywhere as remote as we do. I watch animals dumpster dive all day. My laughing stopped when I saw what was outside. I pulled aside the curtain and could see something very humanlike bending over in the trash can. Humanlike but completely covered in fur. It was not shaped like a bear.

"My breathing must have become heavy because one of my friends could still hear me and was asking me if I was alright. All I said was for them to hold on for a second. As if the creature heard me, it emerged from the garbage can and stared directly into the window. Its eyes were glowing, and its face was hideous. It was like a werewolf, but more manlike than doglike. It stood on its hind legs and looked about seven feet tall, from what I could see. I couldn't take my eyes off it. The creature wiped its mouth of whatever it was tearing into from the garbage but continued staring at me. I couldn't think, and I had forgotten I had my friends on the headset. They were trying to get my attention, but all I could do was stand there thinking that I was seeing things, or that I was going to die. The creature and I both stood there staring at each other. Me feeling complete terror, and the creature just watching.

"I noticed that the Christmas lights from the window were still on, and the tree too. I reached for the plug, not taking my eyes off the Dogman. He looked angry as if me looking at him disturbed his meal. He looked as if he would pounce if I were outside, standing closer to him. I pulled the lights out of the wall; that seemed to startle him. He jumped a bit, knocking over the trash can, making a loud noise. Just then I heard my mother jump out of bed; she must have heard it too. Then the creature took off in the direction of the forest.

"My mother came down the stairs and stared at me silently in shock. She must have seen it too, but didn't know if I had, and didn't want to scare me. My friends were still on the headset, still trying to get my attention. I snapped out of it and told them I had to go, and my mother needed me. We both went outside and picked up the trash the next day. The whole time we didn't say a word to each other. I don't know how much she saw, but I know I saw all of it. I don't like living here anymore. I've already made plans to move down to the city and live with my sister."

Personal note: The witness mentioned bears in her area as a possible suspect. However, because the incident occurred during December, bears are in hibernation for the season, so that would rule them out as a culprit. Another observation that was made was the K-9 was aware that it was being observed by a human from inside the home. This is a common trait among these animals. Maybe it's a survival instinct ability that they have or just a very keen awareness.

NOVEMBER 2000

"I have two cases that happened to me when I was a kid. The first case happened when I was seven back in 2000. Me, my grandfather, and my cousin were driving into my aunt and uncle's driveway at the time in Niskayuna, NY. We drove in, and we saw this big black wolflike creature, and it saw us. This thing was on all four legs and started snarling, very much not afraid of us. It had a bushy tail, as far as I can remember, and it had pointy ears and fangs. We had stayed in the car for however many minutes, and my grandfather honked the horn, and the creature chose to run off. The strange thing about this was that this was in a well-populated area, bunch of houses but more countryside. I remember nothing coming up, no one missing a dog, no reports coming in from anyone else. The creature ran away from us, still growling, but that is all I remember with that case. I wanted to tell you that one.

"This second one was when I was eleven years old and happened back in 2004 in Scotia, NY, where I used to live. I was going outside, and I was playing, just kicking some dirt on the ground, when I looked up and saw this yellow-eyed creature, black as can be, no colors. I was staring at it, and my mom, who was talking to her friend at the time, said to let it be, which I did. The creature had to be as tall as a gray fence, forget what you call them but was tall as that. I could not tell if it was four-legged or two, but I looked at it for however many minutes, ran back into the house to grab a flashlight, and I came back out, and it was still there, just looking at me. I flashed the flashlight on it no luck because it was not a great light at the time. Finally I chose to go inside and just play games.

"Now this is a populated spot, we lived right next door to an old folks home and a bunch of other houses, and they were always out there with the nurses doing whatever, and the strange thing again, no reports, no calls about missing animals.

"However many years later, I had gotten reports that there were a few werewolf encounters in NY the same year. The first, and I don't know if you heard about this encounter, that had happened to a woman driving down a road right next to Lake Champlain; next thing you know, she sees these wolflike creatures on their hind legs, running across the street at what she said, there was two, and they ran to that edge of the lake. Just thought I would share what I thought was interesting, that of my two cases."

LAKE LUZERNE, 1998

"I believe I've had an encounter when I was very young. To this day the image is so ingrained into my mind, and I haven't talked about it much before. I'm unsure of what I really saw and if it was even real at all.

"I was sitting in my living room on the couch with my

back facing the window. It was late at night, and my garden was pitch black (you couldn't make out anything outside). My garden is really big for the area (rural suburbs). Right behind it are railway tracks, and on either side of those are areas of very overgrown vegetation (trees, bushes, long grass), basically heaven for any animals. My back fence is very small, and my neighbor has even had a herd of deer in his back garden before, eating everything in his vegetable garden. We often see rural wildlife: foxes, badgers, hedgehogs, etc.

"I was just sitting there waiting for my food to finish cooking in the oven and on my phone. Next thing I know, there's a sudden small tap on the window behind me. Sounded like a cat jumped up onto the window ledge. I often used to feed a few cats in my area, since I was very young and wanted my own one day. I was obsessed with them. So I turn around, thinking one of them has come to the window to say hello like they sometimes do, and I honestly don't know if what I saw was real.

"It was really huge. I was a small child, but this thing was easily standing at seven to eight feet. My dad's around six feet, and I used his height to estimate. The creature was so black, it melted into the darkness, even though its face was pressed right up against the window behind me. It stared down at me with a snarl on its face. Its eyes were super wide and intense. I was physically unable to look away. If I had to describe its eye color, I would say a dark orange. They weren't bright at all, but really dark; even so, they contrasted against the fur. Its gums were pulled back, and I could see these massive sharp canines. Its ears were so long and pointed I'd describe them as jackal-like, with a long muzzle. I felt like it would have had no problem breaking the window; this thing was practically built of pure muscle, from what I could make out.

"For some reason I did not feel scared when we made eye

contact. It must have been at least a full minute, and neither of us moved. I felt completely frozen in place, but oddly extremely calm at the same time. I felt like I should have nothing to fear, but that feeling also felt wrong considering the expression the creature had on its face. After a minute or two, I blinked, and it moved so fast it seemed to simply disappear back into the darkness. That made me think maybe I had just imagined it.

"But since that evening I was always so scared to go back into the garden. I even moved my rabbits to the front of the garden by the door so I wouldn't have to go to the back by the railway. After that night I always had this strong sense of terror whenever I looked at the overgrown undergrowth behind my small back fence, where the railway was. I got so paranoid and felt like I was being watched. This feeling faded over the years, but even now as an adult I always feel weird going to the back of the garden. I don't know if what I saw was even real, but honestly I hope it was just my imagination.

"But the weirdness doesn't end there. After this encounter, I started seeing this imaginary friend in my dreams, or companion. Again, consider that at the time I was a very young child. This was my first and only type of imaginary friend. Strangely it was very similar to the creature I saw. Only being smaller in size and standing on all fours (more traditionally doglike). Appearance-wise, however, they were both jackal-like with long snouts and long big ears. This companion would follow me around and growl at people who would shortly afterwards either hurt me or betray me in some way. So I began to see it as almost a protector of sorts. Some have suggested I may have been seeing a spirit of some kind, or even had a jinn? The thing that's strange to me is the fact this started soon after my encounter with that other creature at my window. Maybe it was my mind's way of trying to rationalize what I saw? I really don't know. I'm forty-six now and obviously don't see this 'imaginary companion' anymore, but the whole experience has always stuck with me."

Personal note: The witness never told me how old he was at the time of the incident. However, there are many case studies of children inventing imaginary friends to help them cope with traumatic experiences. A study based on interviews of middle school students at high risk for developing behavior problems found that having an imaginary companion was associated with better coping strategies.

SARANAC LAKE, NOVEMBER 2021

"My boyfriend and I were driving back from Plattsburgh, headed towards Saranac Lake right along Route 3. There was nothing unusual about our trip, which we've been on many times. We listened to music and carried on a regular conversation. Just as we were re-entering town, and I mean just as we literally passed the Welcome to Saranac Lake sign, there's a curvy part of the road that slithers along the river. It was just getting dark and not snowing yet in November when the incident occurred.

"As we rounded one of the corners, the first thing to catch our eye was a red glowing eye in the headlights. As the creature noticed us, it slowly turned its head, looking straight at us, both eyes now red glowing and fixed on our car. It looked back up the embankment menacingly as if it were stalking prey and wrote us off as not a threat. The creature itself was crouched low to the ground on all fours and looked to be the length and color of a black panther with the jawline of a wolf. The tail swooped and shaggy. Honestly, it looked even longer than a panther and definitely canine.

"For about ten seconds we were silent in the car when I finally said, 'Um, did you see that?' He replied, 'Absolutely, yes.' With my follow-up question being, 'Black crouched wolf with glowing red eyes and swooped tail?' He nods. 'Mhmm.' We agreed not to talk about it any further just in case it was a skinwalker. The close proximity to our residence filled me with unease, especially since just up the hill from the embankment, there's people's backyards with chickens and pets. I moved a little quicker from the car to my front door that night."

EVIDENCE

Historical evidence for the existence of Bigfoot takes the form of Native American accounts of a wildman of the woods. Depictions are remarkably similar across tribes considering the differing regional circumstances and interpretations. As European settlers pressed westward into the wilderness, they too reported encounters with wildmen, boogars, giant hairy apes, mountain devils, etc. Frontiersmen's accounts were usually spun as sensational newspaper stories that were given little credence.

The best contemporary evidence, our adaptations for walking on two feet, is the footprints that corroborate these stories of wildmen. Something is leaving oversized humanlike footprints. They are either misidentified or the trace of a real undiscovered species. The distinctive anatomy, documented consistently over the past seventy years, is compelling evidence of the latter.

Some of the best evidence for Bigfoot continues to emerge from hikers, hunters, and those who are close to nature. Witnesses claiming to be repeatedly visited by Sasquatch families are becoming more commonplace. Reports of encountering bipedal, hairy, humanlike creatures continue without any sign of slowing. When it comes to evidence, the Patterson film of 1967 still holds the crown as the undisputed champion of a cryptid reality. The Sierra Sounds recorded by Ron Moorehead and Al Berry is an honorable mention, vocalizations below the range of normal human hearing by an unknown animal in North America.

As far as historical evidence, numerous Native American tribes throughout North America recognize Sasquatch as a real being. And it is not just here, it's an international phenomenon. Tribes across the US have descriptions and names for these Bigfoot creatures. Some of these are menacing, like hairy cannibal, Stone Giants, or mountain giants. Other names are more approachable, like the forest people, which describes Bigfoot as a creature that was respected and lived alongside. Knowledge Keepers of the Hoopa tribe of Northern California, for example, list the Seven Sacred Laws, which act as the foundation of the relationship their people have with nature. Each of these laws is visually represented by a real animal.

Legends of these large, hairy manlike beasts can be found all over the world. Since the 1950s, the United States version of this has been "Bigfoot." And since 1976, the FBI has discreetly had a file on the subject. That year, Director Peter Byrne of the Bigfoot Information Center and Exhibition in The Dalles, Oregon, sent the FBI approximately fifteen hairs attached to a tiny piece of skin. Byrne wrote that his organization couldn't identify what kind of animal it came from and was hoping the FBI might analyze it. He also wanted to know if the FBI had analyzed suspected Bigfoot hair before; and if so, what the bureau's conclusion was. At the time, Byrne was one of the more prominent Bigfoot researchers, and in 2019, a lot of people think of Bigfoot as being sort of silly and a joke, while others took the subject more seriously.

Jay Cochran Jr., assistant director of the FBI's scientific and technical services division, wrote back to Byrne that he couldn't find any evidence of the FBI analyzing suspected Bigfoot hair, and that the FBI usually only examined physical evidence related to criminal investigations. Still, it sometimes made exceptions "in the interest of research and scientific inquiry," and Cochran said he'd make such an exception for Byrne.

NEWSPAPER ARCHIVES (SKELETAL REMAINS/GIANT SKELETONS FOUND)

June 25, 1885
Erie County Giants
"Skeletons of Men Ten Feet High Found in a Cave"
Philadelphia Times

"Why, this man was ten or twelve feet high!"
"Thunder and lightning!" exclaimed farmer Porter in astonishment. The first speaker who has won local distinction as a scientist, reiterated his assertion.
J.H. Porter has a farm near Northeast Erie County, PA. Not many miles from the Lake Shore Railroad crosses the New York state boundary line. Last week some workmen in Mr. Porters employee came upon the entrance to a cave, and on entering it, found heaps of bones within. Many skeletons were complete, and exhibited to the naturalists and archaeologists of the neighborhood. They informed the wondering bystanders that the remains were unmistakably those of giants. The entire village of Northeast was aroused by the discovery, and Sunday hundreds of people from Erie took advantage of their holiday visit to the scene.
It was first conjectured that the remains were those of soldiers killed in battle with Indians that abounded in the

vicinity during the last century, but the size of the skulls and the length of the leg bones dispelled the theory. So far about a hundred and fifty giant skeletons of powerful proportions have been exhumed and indications point to a second cave eastward, which may probably contain as many more. Scientists who have exhumed skeletons and made careful measurements of the bones say they are a race of gigantic creatures, compared with which our tallest men would appear as pigmies. There are now arrowheads, stone hatchets or other implements of war with the bodies. Some of the bones are on exhibition at various stores. One is as thick as a good sized bucket.

June 12, 1888
Indians Were Giants Then
Chicago Tribune

LOCKPORT, N.Y. June 9. On the farm of William Squires in the Village of Gorman, Ontario County, is a high mound on which a barn was erected about seventy years ago. About a year ago Mr. Squires, in making an excavation for a new foundation for his barn, found some bones. The Rev. John W. Sanborn of this city heard of it and obtained ten skeletons. Mr. Sanborn took a skull, a backbone, leg bones, arm and finger bones to England with him to illustrate his paper which he read there. In the largest skeleton the femur was nineteen inches long. The man must have been between seven and eight feet tall. The skull was one of the ugliest and most brutal looking ever seen. It was probably a burying ground of the Seneca Nation, and the find is a most important one. Some of the skeletons will be sent to the Anatomical Museum of Cambridge University in England.

July 24, 1891
Skeleton Giants
"Prehistoric Couple Found Side by Side, but the Woman's Jaw Gave Way First."

CHAUTAUQUA, N.Y., July 23. In grading for an electric railroad to connect Lakewood and Jamestown two day laborers plowed up, near Lakewood, the bones of a man and woman of remarkable size. Local historians claim that they are the remains of a prehistoric race. Whatever the real facts may be, the affair has caused much excitement in this section, and everybody has a theory for the skeleton giants. One newspaper man here brought home the femur and skull of the man in a flour sack, and has them on exhibition at Chautauqua tonight. The current belief is that they were white settlers who fell in the French and Indian wars. A very curious and suggestive thing about the "find" was that the lower jaw of the man was intact while that of the woman was entirely gone, showing that woman kind was much the same in prehistoric times as now.

April 27, 1898
Curious Skeletons Found

Arm of one indicates a man seven feet high, the skull's odd protuberances.

While workmen were excavating for the Toledo and Ottawa Beach railway recently they unearthed a bed of old pottery and a number of skeletons. The point where the discovery was made is about 1, 1 to 3 miles from the city limits of Toledo, on the city side of Ottawa creek. The contractors found a ridge, or mound, on the proposed line of the road and were compelled to dig through it.

In the solid yellow clay, at a depth of about eight feet, they came across the relics. Three skeletons, undoubtedly of aborigines, were brought to the surface, and an arm, evidently of a giant, was among the bones. It was in a good state of preservation and had belonged to a man fully 7 feet in height. While the workmen were digging out other relics, some farmer picked up the arm and made off with it. A strange feature of the discovery is that none of the skeletons are perfect. Bones are entirely missing from all of them. The skulls are curious. On two of them, just where the edge of the ears would come on either side, are bony protuberances which curl forward, not unlike horns. Several tomahawks have been picked up. New York Tribune.

A HISTORY OF LIVINGSTON COUNTY, NEW YORK, 1824

When Jesse Stanley came to Mount Morris in 1811, an Indian mound nearly one hundred feet in diameter and from eight to ten feet high covered the site of the late General Mills residence. The mound had been crowned by a great tree, which had recently fallen under the ax. Deacon Stanley was told that when freshly cut, it disclosed 130 concentric circles or yearly growths.

About the year 1820, the mound was removed, and in its removal, arrowheads, a brass kettle, and knives were thrown out. A number of skeletons were also disinterred. Among the bones was a human skeleton of enormous size, the jawbone of which was so large that Adam Holslander placed it, mask like, over his own chin and jaw. He was the largest man in the settlement, and his face was in proportion to the rest of his body. Metal in the form of rude medals, a pipe and other articles were picked out of the earth thrown from the excavation.

A HISTORY OF WESTERN NEW YORK, 1804

Human bones of gigantic proportion were discovered in such a state of preservation as to be accurately described and measured. The cavities of the skulls were large enough in their dimensions to receive the entire head of a man of modern times, and could be put on one's head with as much ease as a hat or cap. The jawbones were sufficiently large to admit to being placed so as to match or fit outside of a modern man's face. The other bones so far discovered appear to be of equal proportion with the skull and jawbones, several of which have been preserved in the cabinets of antiquarians, where they still may be seen.

ROCHESTER, 1796

A natural sand mound revealed a surprise in 1796. "On the shore of Lake Ontario on a high bluff near Irondequoit Bay ... the bank caved off and untombed a great quantity of human bones of a large size," observed Rochester resident Oliver Culver. A number of sources preserve his account, including Turner's *History of the Pioneer Settlement of the Phelps and Gorham Purchase* (1851). "As late as 1830 human bones of an unusually large size were occasionally seen projecting from the face of the bluff or lying on the beach," reported G. H. Harris in *Aboriginal Occupation of the Lower Genesee County* (1884). "The arm and leg bones, upon comparison, were much larger than those of our own race," wrote Arthur Caswell Parker in *The Archaeological History of New York* (1922). By that I think the great Seneca scholar meant "the human race." I doubt that a thorough excavation was ever made here. If the local landscaping hasn't been too dramatic, some bones could still be left. FYI, I hear this spot was on the west side of Irondequoit Bay.

Discoveries of the giant skeletons were found all over the northeast, from Martha's Vineyard and Deerfield Valley, Massachusetts, to Vermont and Upstate New York. Other reports of the discovery of buried giants were also found in the South, Midwest and West Coast. In the Ohio River Valley, a report from a local paper, which was backed up by *Scientific American*, found bodies of several giants buried under a ten-foot-tall mound. One female skeleton was found holding a three-and-a-half-foot-long child. Another of the giant skeletons was buried in a clay coffin, and an engraved stone tablet was also recovered. This particular mound was sixty-four feet long by thirty-five feet wide. The history books deny that giants existed! Although so much evidence exists pointing towards the fact that giants once walked the planet.

1. Large bones in stone graves in Williamson County and White County, Tennessee. Discovered in the early 1800s, the average stature of these giants was seven feet tall.

2. Giant skeletons found in the mid-1800s in New York State near Rutland and Rodman.

3. In 1833, soldiers digging at Lompock Rancho, California, discovered a male skeleton twelve feet tall. The skeleton was surrounded by carved shells, stone axes, and other artifacts. The skeleton had double rows of upper and lower teeth. Unfortunately, this body was secretly buried because the local Indians became upset about the remains.

4. A giant skull and vertebrae found in Wisconsin and Kansas City.

5. A giant found off the California coast on Santa Rosa Island in the 1800s was distinguished by its double rows of teeth.

6. A nine-foot, eight-inch skeleton was excavated from a mound near Brewersville, Indiana, in 1879.

7. Skeletons of "enormous dimensions" were found in mounds near Zanesville, Ohio, and Warren, Minnesota, in the 1880s.

8. In Clearwater, Minnesota, the skeletons of seven giants were found in mounds. These had receding foreheads and complete double dentition.

9. At Le Crescent, Wisconsin, mounds were found to contain giant bones. Five miles north near Dresbach, the bones of people over eight feet tall were found.

10. In 1888 seven skeletons ranging from seven to eight feet tall were discovered.

11. Near Toledo, Ohio, twenty skeletons were discovered with jaws and teeth "twice as large as those of present day people." The account also noted that odd hieroglyphics were found with the bodies.

12. Miners in Lovelock Cave, California, discovered a very tall, red-haired mummy in 1911.

13. This mummy eventually went to a fraternal lodge, where it was used for "initiation purposes."

14. In 1931, skeletons from eight and a half to ten feet long were found in the Humbolt lake bed in California.

15. In 1932, Ellis Wright found human tracks in the gypsum rock at White Sands, New Mexico. His discovery was later backed up by Fred Arthur, supervisor of the Lincoln National Park, and others who reported that each footprint was

twenty-two inches long and from eight to ten inches wide. They were certain the prints were human in origin due to the outline of the perfect prints coupled with a readily apparent instep.

16. During World War II, author Ivan T. Sanderson tells of how his crew was bulldozing through sedimentary rock when they stumbled upon what appeared to be a graveyard. In it were crania that measured from twenty-two to twenty-four inches from base to crown, nearly three times as large as an adult human skull. Had the creatures to whom these skulls belonged been properly proportioned, they undoubtedly would have been at least twelve feet tall or taller.

17. In 1947 a local newspaper reported the discovery of nine-foot-tall skeletons by amateur archeologists working in Death Valley.

18. The archeologists involved also claimed to have found what appeared to be the bones of tigers and dinosaurs with the human remains.

19. The Catalina Islands, off California, are the home of dwarf mammoth bones that were once roasted in ancient firepits. These were roasted and eaten by humanlike creatures who were giants with double rows of teeth.

An 1890 *New York Times* article has been unearthed that describes the stunning archaeological discovery of "a race of Indian giants," and about fifty skeletons of Indians were found at an Indian graveyard near Edgewater Avenue in Pleasantville, with many of them measuring seven feet tall and one measuring eight feet tall.

A RACE OF INDIAN GIANTS

MAY'S LANDING, FEBRUARY 9

For over a week past crowds have been flocking to the site of the unearthed Indian graveyard near Edgewater in Pleasantville. The first lot of skeletons unearthed was about one thousand yards from the city post office and embraced eight bodies, closely laid together in a deep chamber snugly packed in with tortoise, oyster and clam shells. One of this number had bead and shell decorations, which together with its extreme height, points to the fact that it must have been the powerful old Chief Kineawauga, whose descendants still own farms along the shore.

Professor C. H. Farrel of Baltimore, Charlie K. Simpson of New York, John H. Cooley of New Haven Connecticut and several gentlemen from the University of Pennsylvania immediately went to the scene. Mr. Rialey and Farr, the owners of the land, gave to the Archaeological Association of the University of Pennsylvania the right to search for relics on their land. These researchers have been watched by thousands of people with great interest. Besides weapons of war, savage ornamental war decorations and numerous valuable shells, stones, etc. Over fifty skeletons have been excavated.

Dr. Charles R. Abbot, curator of the association, is continuing the search, and the skeletons are to be shipped to the university at once. They run in size from a small child to several of seven feet in height, and one supposed to be an old medicine man. Wauneck must have been at least eight feet in height. About fifty students were upon the ground this morning and continued their search until stopped by rain.

The citizens gaze in silent wonder on these relics of a race that at one time ruled the land. For seven miles along the shore can be seen large mounds of clam and oyster shells left here by Indians who used to congregate by hundreds to open oysters for winter food, and it's near these shell mounds that the great number of skeletons have been taken up. In some instances weapons of war made of stone and flint have been found lying close beside some exceedingly large skeletons. The relics will be put on exhibition at the museum of the University of Pennsylvania.

IN THE FALL OF 1869

A farmer named Stub Newell asked some neighbors to come over to help dig a well on his property in Upstate New York, near the tiny town of Cardiff. When they broke ground, not far beneath the surface, they hit something hard.

Soon, they had uncovered something incredible: a giant stone man. The giant weighed almost three thousand pounds and was ten feet tall. Newell and his neighbors weren't quite sure what it was – a petrified man or an ancient statue? Either way, people were interested. They came from miles around to see the Cardiff Giant, and Newell started charging fifty cents per person. Now, ten feet is awfully tall for a human being: even today, the tallest person ever measured was just under nine feet tall. And soon enough it became clear that the giant found on Newell's farm wasn't real.

Very few scientists ever believed the giant was actually a petrified man although some did buy the ancient statue story. But in reality, he had been carved just a year or so before. George Hull, Newell's cousin, had heard a Protestant preacher talking about the biblical account of giants roaming the earth, and had seen an opportunity. In secret, he had the giant made from a giant block of gypsum, arranged for it to be buried on Newell's land, and then waited.

The truth about the giant came out within a few months of its discovery. By that point, Hull and Newell had already sold their giant (now at the Farmers' Museum, in Cooperstown, NY), and P. T. Barnum had made a plaster copy (now at Marvin's Marvelous Mechanical Museum, in Michigan). The Cardiff Giant was far from the only giant that's been discovered over the years. In the 1870s, another Hull-created giant showed up in Colorado. A few years after that, a hotel in Upstate New York found their own petrified giant. In 1890, a French anthropologist discovered a set of giant bones that he insisted was human. A few years after that, a saloon in Colorado was giving people a look at a concrete giant named McGinty for an admission price of one dollar a person. People want giants to be real so badly that some believe the Smithsonian Institute has actively covered up evidence of giants' existence.

TREE STRUCTURES

On numerous occasions, researchers like me have reported finding curious creations in areas where there is a high number of reported Bigfoot activity. Essentially, they are teepee-like structures and other anomalous shapes that appear to have been created by something with intelligence, and a great feat of strength. As for why these hairy hominids might choose to engage in such behavior, the theories are several.

At first glance, one might assume they have been constructed to offer themselves adequate shelter, particularly during the cold winter months. In many cases, there does not appear to have been any attempt made to create a canopy or walls. Therefore, the structures are open to the environment and all of its attendant harshness. Other theories are that it has been speculated that the teepees represent territorial markers created by a Sasquatch creature to alert the others of their kind that they are present in the area. They may also be a warning to man to stay away; the obscure nature of the formations could mean that very few of us are likely to understand such a warning, let alone act on it.

Sudbury Vt 2020

Sudbury Vt 2020

Castleton, VT 2016

Castleton, VT 2016

Buck Mountain, NY 2017

Sabath Day Point NY 2015

Whitehall NY 2018

Bennington VT 2019

FOOTPRINTS

After examining various footprints and casts, I have identified some key clues that reveal the skeletal anatomy of the foot and its joints, proportions and dynamic interactions with the ground. Each cast or footprint has the potential of adding an additional piece to the puzzle, or to further substantiate an inference about the functional anatomy of the Sasquatch foot. Rather than simply an enlarged human foot, the hominid's foot displays a unique combination of more primitive apelike features combined with human specializations for bipedalism. The prospect of a large primate that may have independently evolved bipedalism is intriguing in several respects, including a better understanding of primate diversity and the origin of human adaptations.

The footprint of a Sasquatch hominid is much larger than a human footprint and has features that are much more distinct. Their foot has an elongated heel, which is considerably higher up on the foot than an average human heel. Front tracks of Bigfoot can be differentiated from human footprints in several ways. For instance, the ergonomics of the foot, such as radius and ulna length-to-width ratios and toe lengths, are distinctly different between humans and Bigfoot. The positions of metatarsal heads at heel contact also differ; for humans, they will be under the ground. Their toes are wider than their feet, while human toes conform more to the shape of the foot.

Among the factors that scientists use to identify a Bigfoot footprint from human footprints are the length and width, depth, impression level, toe spread, and heel imprint. Bigfoot prints usually ooze far more mud than human ones, and they also tend to be indisputable with their size and depth. A Bigfoot footprint can be identified from a human footprint by looking at the thickness of the heel. The heel on a Bigfoot print will be much wider than that of a human; the ankle is shifted forward a few inches; the foot has no arch because no arch will support that kind of weight. And the Bigfoot will also have a longer stride length.

It is also possible to identify a Bigfoot footprint from human footprints by looking at the length of the toes. Assuming that these hominids are closer to the human scale, calculating the height of these hominids can be determined by taking the length of the foot in inches and multiplying that number by 6.6. That will give the height of the subject in inches. These variant features are exactly what you would expect to find in a foot that was designed to support the weight of a six-hundred-plus-pound being. These are completely redesigned feet because they are completely redesigned creatures.

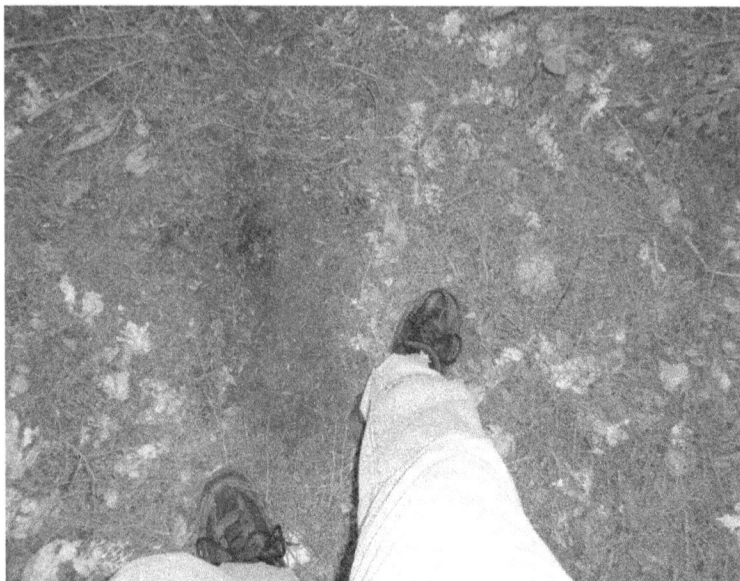

Buck Mountain, NY 2017

Stoney Creek NY 2015

Inman Pond NY 2018

West Mountain NY 2019. Photo courtesy of Brian Gosselin

Castleton VT 2022

MIDTARSAL BREAK

The midtarsal break was first described in this journal nearly seventy-five years ago to explain the ability of nonhuman primates to lift their heel independently of the rest of the foot. Since the initial description of the midtarsal break, the calcaneocuboid joint has been assumed to be the anatomical source of this motion. Recently, however, it has been suggested that the midtarsal break may occur at the cuboid-metatarsal joint rather than at the calcaneocuboid joint. Data compiled from X-rays, dissections, manual manipulation of living primate feet, video of captive catarrhines, and osteological specimens concur that the midtarsal break is a complex motion caused by dorsiflexion at both joints with the cuboid-metatarsal joint contributing roughly two-thirds of total midfoot dorsiflexion, and the calcaneocuboid joint only about one-third of total midfoot dorsiflexion. The convexity of the proximal articular surface of the fourth and fifth metatarsals and corresponding concave cuboid facets provide skeletal correlates for the presence of midfoot dorsiflexion at the cuboid-metatarsal joint. Study of hominin metatarsals from *Australopithecus afarensis*, *A. africanus*, *Homo erectus*, and the metatarsals and a cuboid from the OH 8 foot show little capacity for dorsiflexion at the cuboid-metatarsal joint. These results suggest that hominins may have already evolved a stable midfoot region well adapted for the push-off phase of bipedalism by at least 3.2 million years ago. These data illuminate the evolution of the longitudinal arch and show further evidence of constraints on the arboreal capacity in early hominins.

(In simpler terms), a human has a longitudinal arch, which means the entire foot is incorporated into the lever that propels it off the ground, and weight is pushed to the ball of the foot. The bending happens at the toes, providing traction. In a foot with midfoot flexibility, the weight is not concentrated on the ball of the foot, but rather the midfoot. Midfoot flexibility causes weight to transfer from rear to forefront and is most commonly present in apes. This anatomy shows itself in the form of a midtarsal break within footprints. The midtarsal break is a feature of the print that occurs when the midfoot bends, causing the dirt or sand to lift up into a small mound in the middle of the footprint. Other great apes have a divergent big toe, which is used for climbing. Humans and Sasquatch have transitioned to bipedalism, causing their big toe to align with the other toes as their need for climbing trees has diminished.

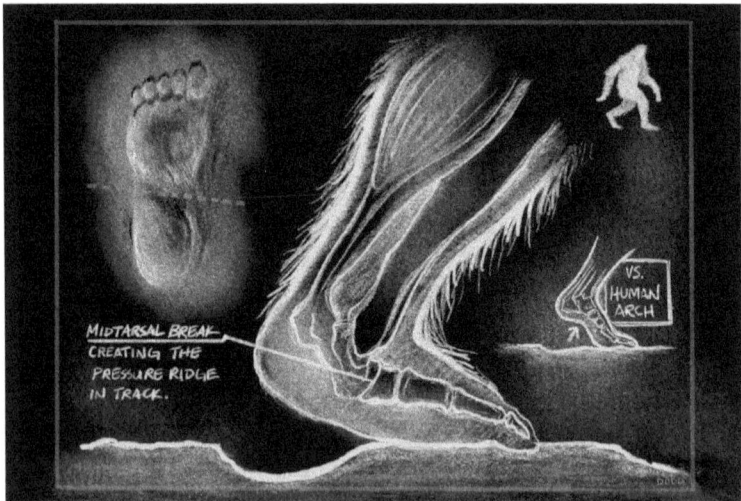

Illustration of mid foot flexibility

NESTS

Many theories among researchers have suggested that these hominids use nest like structures when they bed down for the night. Many know African primates share this same behavior.

Found nest structure in Brant Lake NY 2016

Emily of The Forest Fleur writes:

"Evidence strongly suggests that Sasquatch sleeps on the ground just like us humans. The Olympic Project of Washington has documented several nesting sites containing over 20 ground nests that resemble those of known apes & measure between 4-9 feet. Between credible eye-witness reports, ground nesting sites & no evidence of nesting in trees, we can conclude that Sasquatch spends their time sleeping on the ground.

"According to *Why We Sleep* by Matthew Walker, English scientist & professor of neuroscience & psychology at the University of California, Berkeley, sleep is essential to intelligence, memory function, & evolution. Why are we smarter than other primates? It may just have something to do with sleep. REM, or Rapid Eye Movement sleep, is a deep paralysis that boosts social complexity & cognitive intelligence.

Because primates sleep in trees, they cannot achieve REM sleep, as the sleep paralysis would cause them to fall to their death.

"While other hominoids were sleeping in trees, *Homo erectus* (our ancestor) learned how to make fire, allowing them to sleep safely on the ground & reach REM sleep. This change in sleeping patterns could be what evolved *Homo sapiens* intelligence. Humans spend 20–25% of our sleep in the REM state, compared to a 9% average across other primates. Other apes sleep longer, but we sleep deeper, leaving us more time for social learning & innovation!

" What does this mean? If modern humans evolved our social complexity & cognitive intelligence through REM sleep, Sasquatch may have too!"

HAIR SAMPLES

In addition to footprints, hair samples have also been analyzed and determined to originate from an unknown hominid. Dr. Jeff Meldrum and Dr. Henner Fahrenbach examined unknown hair samples to determine their origin. In order to identify a species, scientists observe overlapping scales, which can be different in color and thickness, diameter of the hair, cross-sectional shape, and length of the hair shaft. Human hair grows differently and longer than other species, therefore showing characteristics such as a cut end and distinctive follicle structure. After Fahrenbach gathered nearly a dozen samples that were not linked to any known animal, the two scientists began studying their similarities.

After a five-year study of more than one hundred DNA samples from all over North America, a research team from Texas has concluded that the creature may be a human relative that somehow developed around fifteen thousand years ago as a result of a hybrid cross between *Homo sapiens* with an unknown primate. Their team consists of experts in genetics, forensics, imaging and pathology. The researchers said they believe that over the past five years, the team has successfully found three Sasquatch nuclear genomes, an organism's hereditary code, leading them to suggest that the animal is real and a human hybrid.

The team's study showed that part of the DNA the team sequenced revealed an unknown primate species, which suggests that Bigfoot is a real creature that resulted from this primate "crossing with female *Homo sapiens*." The fact is, nearly every DNA test done in association with Bigfoot hair samples has come back as human. When you come to the realization that Bigfoot is a human hybrid, then you start to open the doors to other unusual giant-sized humans in our past.

5 TYPES OF BIGFOOT

The type 1 (AKA the Patty type). This is the classic Sasquatch. It looks like a cross between a human and a mountain gorilla. It has a large powerful build, a thick broad chest, dark brown to black hair, and dark skin. Other hair colors reported are brown, auburn, cinnamon, and occasionally white or blonde. The head, though massive, has been described as relatively small for the body. Type 1 sometimes develops a sagittal crest, which can look like a person wearing a hoodie, also referred to as a conical head. They have a pronounced brow ridge with a receding forehead, giving the eyes a deep-set look. The eyes are often large and black like those of an owl and are known to glow red in complete darkness. This is speculated as some form of night-vision ability. Type 1 has a flat face with prominent cheekbones and a square jaw. The mouth region is only slightly protuberant.

The nose is near human in shape, though pug or flat, sometimes with forward-directed nostrils. The height average for the sampled population is from seven to ten feet in height. However, alpha males have been reported at nine feet and larger. Its weight is estimated to weigh in between five hundred and eight hundred pounds.

The Type 2 (AKA wood boogers) appears more apelike than the type 1. They're reported in many areas of North America, but especially in the south and in swamp and creek areas. Type 2 have a bestial manlike build and large eyes with large pupil dilations for night vision. The hair is often reported as black, but auburn, orange, and light brown have been reported. A bit smaller than type 1, the average height is around seven feet. Type 2s tend to be very territorial and can be aggressive. They favor killing livestock, especially the smaller varieties such as goats and chickens. Type 2s leave three-toed footprints but can be very much like known primates such as chimps and orangutans.

The Type 3 is something like a mandrill-human mix. They look similar to a Bigfoot, but more savage or vicious. Descriptions of the face vary, but most reports describe a large dog/bear/baboon-faced bipedal mammal. Type 3 can be extremely tall, between ten to fifteen feet reported, with oversized heads that look more monster-like than ape. They tend to live up in the mountains, but will come down for food. The hair is typically dark or deep brown. One witness reported seeing a type 3 wearing animal pelts over their hair. They may eat humans, but reports of man-eating are rare and often based on old legends. Type 3s tend to incite reports of paranormal characteristics, like having glowing red eyes or being bulletproof at close range. Type 3s are also known to live up in the colder climates such as Alaska, but are not known to be in the Adirondacks.

The Type 4 reports often come from the north/northeast. They have been referred to as "early man Bigfoot" and the American almas. They are the most human looking of the hairy bipedal humanoids, possessing traits of archaic/prehistoric man. They're typically a bit leaner than the type 1s, but are still large and well muscled. A hairy *Homo heidelbergensis* is a decent model for the type 4. They have less facial hair than the other types. The crown of the head can have thinning hair or even be bald. Some eyewitnesses have reported beards and mustaches ranging from noticeable to full grown. Type 4s have round heads (not conical). Their noses are hooded. The mouth is wider than what we would consider normal. The teeth are square and human looking. The skin color can be pasty gray to black with a leathery appearance. Some people think these are hybrids, part human, part primate. They might just be; however, all members of the genus *Homo* developed and used tools at some point. There are no reports of these type 4s using tools of any kind.

The Type 5, the Genoskwa, is a subspecies of Sasquatch mentioned by Native Americans as the "Stone Giant Man." In Iroquois legend, this hairy hominid was known as "otneyarhed" or "otneyarheh," which also translates to "Stone Giant" or "Stonecoat." It is reported as Sasquatch's larger, bulkier and more aggressive cousin and is very violent when encountered. It has rock-hard skin, and they twist the heads of their victims until they are decapitated. It is also known to throw rocks at people. They are said to be much more aggressive than most other Sasquatches and appear to be very violent and territorial. It is about nine to eleven feet tall and 800-1,030 pounds. The hair color is a dark brown or black. The eyes are large and black with a very angry appearance. The mouth is wide with large square human-looking teeth and a flat nose.

An explanation for how the creatures got this name could be that their fur was often coarsened with dirt or mud after rolling around in it, which would later harden and look like stone or possibly an outer layer of armor protection, possibly against arrows. With this standing as a possible theory, it could be said the Genoskwa may have been no different from the typical Sasquatch (slightly different in temperament) save for the fact they were covered in mud. Aside from the "armor" aspect of the Genoskwa creature, the Genoskwa are also said to exude a horrible odor from their armpits that is described as a mixture between that of a skunk and a dead animal.

THE VERMONT SIDE OF THINGS

Although Vermont is not considered part of the Adirondacks, I felt it was necessary to include this chapter due to the migration patterns of these hominids that move from New York and into Vermont. Biologist John Perry of Maine reported that sightings of Bigfoot in New England should be viewed as a collection of incidences throughout a vast area rather than just limiting the creature to one state. After all, they don't know about our borders much less care about them, so they roam where they will, crossing state lines without notice. He makes a good point, especially as I contemplated the sightings and reports from Vermont in recent years; they seem to tie in with reports just over the border in the state of New York.

Sightings of Bigfoot date back to the Colonial era in those areas, and the Native Americans knew about them, referring to them as wildmen or Stone Giants. The areas where Bigfoot have been spotted stretch from northern Albany, New York, through Crown Point on Lake Champlain in Vermont. But that entire Adirondack region contains over six million acres of state park, so a Bigfoot population could move about fairly freely and thrive.

A noted backwoods country guy known as "Adirondack" Jack Leach was interviewed about his encounters with Bigfoot. With over fifty years of experience roaming the wilderness while hunting and fishing, Jack had quite a few stories to tell. He seems genuine and certainly seems to be a levelheaded sort of person. I found his claims to be believable.

The FBI this week released over twenty pages of official agency records pertaining to Bigfoot in the United States. While the FBI files make no mention of Vermont, some, like Frank Siecienski of Hubbardton, think the creatures could be wandering around the woods of Vermont. Siecienski, a self-described Bigfoot and Sasquatch researcher, said he has proof to back up his claims that Vermont is a great place for these creatures to live. Along with the hundreds of requests received last year to protect more well-known plants and animals, the US Fish and Wildlife Service was queried about protection for Bigfoot and the Lake Champlain sea serpent.

In September 2010, Siecienski said he caught an image of a Bigfoot on a trail camera that was stationed on part of his property in Hubbardton. Bigfoot sightings in Vermont date back to the late '70s into the early '80s if not later, Siecienski said, and include sightings by a professor from Castleton University and his daughter. Vermont is a prime location for Bigfoot and Sasquatch because it's so remote and has a lot of undisturbed private property, Siecienski said. Places like Rutland and Hubbardton consistently have sightings due to the woods and remoteness of parts of the area, he said. "Some people do believe, and others don't believe," Siecienski said. "I do believe."

February 28, 1882
Boston Weekly Globe
"A STRANGE ANOMALY."
A female covered with hair running untamed in the woods at
Stamford, VT.

BENNINGTON, VT., February 25, A Frenchman who recently visited a place called the "Bear Swamp," near Stamford, VT, on a hunting excursion, related this story, and furnished partial proof of his statement in the scars which his physiolognomy bears:

After traveling about the woods in the vicinity of the "Bear Swamp" with varying success for about half an hour, he was startled by a sudden noise in the thicket nearby, and at once put his gun to his shoulder, but seeing a strange appearance, which at first sight he imagined a bear, he started on run for a tree. A wild, maniacal laugh followed him, and the black, hairy creature disappeared walking, as deponent thought, on its hind legs. The noise emitted from the creature's lungs led the hunter to believe that it was something other than a bear, and mustering as much temerity as his frightened condition would allow, he started to investigate. He had proceeded but a short distance into the depths of the brush and undergrowth, where he caught sight of the black figure leaning over a spring drinking, its back towards the hunter. The time had arrived for action, and throwing down his gun the hunter rushed to the creature, clasping his arms around what proved to be the waist of a woman, nude, except for the heavy growth of black hair that covered every portion of her body, except a part of her breast. The hug was but temporary, however, for turning upon him, the strange creature pierced and tore the inquisitive hunter's faced till he was glad to let go and run for his life. The crazy, sepulchral laugh followed him, however, and the hunter will avoid in the future this to him decidedly unpleasant locality.

THE TOWN OF ROCKINGHAM, VERMONT, 1907

When the earth was removed from the top of the ledges east of the falls, a remarkable human skeleton, unmistakably that of an Indian, was found. Those who saw it tell the writer that the jawbone was of such size that a large man could easily slip it over his face, and the teeth, which were all double, were perfect. This skeleton was kept for many years deposited in the attic of a small building on the north side of the square. This building was then occupied by Dr. John H. Wells' office and drug store and stood where the Italian fruit store now does. When the building was rebuilt a decade ago or more, the bones disappeared.

RICHMOND, VT, JULY 2021

One night, after a night at the bars, I got home around 2:30 a.m. When I got out of my car, I heard this God-awful howl. It actually was between a howl and a scream, coming from what I thought was the school across the street. I listened, then decided that I didn't feel safe. This went on for about three weeks. Every time I was out late coming home, I would hear it.

The last time I heard the howl was when it came from a lot of land about one acre in size behind the three last houses on our street. Then I heard the trees starting to really shake, and that's when I ran into the house. Haven't heard it since, but with covid, the bar has been closed, so I don't go out that late. And in case some wonder, I have a beer in the span of the five hours that I'm at the bar. I have pop and coffee after that beer.

The street that my house is on has six houses on it, with a school across from us and a playground at the end. The acre of land behind us used to belong to an old man who kept goats many, many years ago. Nothing is left, so trees have grown up. There's also a creek running through it ...

Update ... four nights ago I was sitting in my living room when all of a sudden I heard a scream coming from behind the house. It was so loud that I thought it was coming from inside the house. Didn't think much of it except that it was an animal of some sort. As I said, the original howl was two years ago, so that was the last thing on my mind. So I made sure the doors were locked and went to bed.

BURLINGTON FREE PRESS, VERMONT, AUGUST 3, 1910

Is it, or is it not the real wildman walking around the New Burlington? A real sure enough wildman has been discovered in a South Burlington blueberry swamp. At least so it's alleged. A man in that vicinity blew into Burlington yesterday and sat on a bench in city hall park where he incidentally met a free press reporter and told a weird tale about a man of enormous size covered with bristling red hair who had been seen several times at a swamp near South Burlington. The wild man, if that's what it is, was first seen by a little girl picking berries. She had a large bucket and a small one. When she filled the small pail, she went to the big one and emptied the contents. After several trips she noticed that the big bucket didn't seem to be filling up as it should have been. So she concealed herself in the bushes and watched. After a few moments, a man of enormous stature almost entirely covered in red hair and carrying only a gunny sack appeared, and after glancing about, he began to eat the berries by hand. The little girl was frightened, needless to say. And after the creature had eaten her berries, the little girl took the pail and ran home.

But there are other evidence of the wildman's existence. Sheep had been found in the neighborhood of several pastures of South Burlington horribly mangled. And the good housewives of that suburb have been missing canned fruit and other goodies which could have been extracted through a pantry window. There are a lot of shotguns loaded in South Burlington, and it's safe to say that if the wildman makes his appearance in daylight near human habitation, he'll have a good size charge of lead injected into his system.

NORTHFIELD FALLS. NOVEMBER 2015

"On two separate mornings while deer hunting in a fairly remote section of Washington County, before sunrise, and after tree breaks and knocks at close range, something screamed/whooped at me. I am a Vermont native, grew up hunting, camping, fishing, and generally immersed in the outdoors, and while I am familiar with the subject of Bigfoot, I have never experienced anything like this before or since.

"The conditions on both mornings were clear, cold, and extremely quiet. I had hiked into where I was going to hunt, leaving my vehicle around 5:00 a.m., getting to where I wanted to sit around 5:45 a.m., and after changing into my dry underlayers, had shut my light off and settled into wait for first light. Activity began both mornings only minutes after dousing my light. This occurred in November of last fall, 2015."

This spring a man from Waitsfield, the next town over, posted on his front porch forum that while hiking on the vast trail in the Southwest Basin on Waitsfield Mountain, he had observed a tall, hairy, bipedal creature dragging a dead goat by its horns up into the cliff band. He advised that if you were in the area to be cautious.

Personal note: The area of Northfield, Vermont, is home to the legendary "pigman" encounters back in the 1970s. Most of which took place in an area known as "the Devil's Washbowl." The "pigman" of Northfield, Vermont, is a legend that has been passed down through the years in the town of Northfield. According to the story, the pigman was a humanoid creature that was half-man and half-pig and was said to roam the woods and fields of Northfield. The pigman is often told as a tale to young children, warning them not to wander off into the woods alone. Some versions of the story say that the pigman would kidnap or harm anyone who crossed his path, while others claim that he was simply a mischievous and playful creature. I wrote a lengthy article on pigman in my previous book Vermont Bigfoot Encounters and Beyond, describing eyewitness encounters.

EDEN, 2013

"I live in the small town of Eden. Not much goes on out here. Maybe a few coyotes or bears once in a while. When my daughter was five years old, during the summer of 2013, she started telling me about her friend that she named 'big hairy man.' At first I thought she had an imaginary friend. Most kids do at her age. She talked about him constantly, almost daily. When I asked about him, she said that he lives in the woods. I thought that it might be a homeless man and that she should stay away from him. From that day, I kept a closer eye on her when she was in the backyard just to be safe.

"One day in August of that year, I was downstairs doing laundry when she came running in the house frantically. She said big hairy man was back. I asked what was wrong, and she replied, 'I don't like big hairy man; he's throwing pinecones at me.' I ran outside to see who was out there, but I didn't see anyone. I thought I may have heard some rummaging in the woods, but I wasn't sure. Maybe I'm overreacting, or maybe there's something out there in these woods, taunting my little daughter."

Personal note: The mother reached out to me in 2020 through social media, and we corresponded through email. I eventually talked to her over the phone, but due to the covid scare, she wasn't comfortable having any visitors at that time. During our phone interview, her daughter gave a description of her friend as being very tall, well over six feet maybe seven, and covered in dark brown hair from head to toe. The kid was very descriptive about facial features and described him as having "big owl eyes." This is another classic case of a child interacting with a Sasquatch creature.

BRATTLEBORO, ROUTE 9, OCTOBER 17, 2015

"About 5:30 a.m. on Route 9 headed into West Brattleboro, VT, my husband and I saw a small (I don't know what) running across the road. It was about three to four feet tall, long dark brown to black hair, running on two legs. I caught the animal in my headlights very clearly. The one thing we both said was that it was fast. Faster than any animal we have ever seen. It was crossing the road into the swampy area near the small whetstone brook. There were tall reeds there, and it disappeared into them. We did not stop. In retrospect, I wish I had. It might have answered some questions we both had."

EDEN, AUGUST 2019

"I am sixty-seven, a retired RN and former private pilot with excellent vision, 20/15, so I was not mistaken. It was not a bear. We have had a bear here by the deck, so I know what bears look like standing up to reach the feeder. It was a sunny day; my small Chihuahua mix was out front in her cage. She was barking, so I walked out to the front deck and looked towards the dirt road where she was looking. We sat back approximately 125 feet from the road. I saw a very black-looking humanoid shape walking on two legs go past our driveway. It was half bent over, then straightened up. It had long arms swinging. The head was turned away and appeared to have a very short neck and roundish head from that angle. I said to myself, 'That looks like a chimp!'

"I watched it for approximately twelve seconds until it disappeared behind the trees, going east. There are spots that I can see through the trees to the neighbor's drive, so I was looking for it to either go up the drive or continue on the road. When it did not, I walked out to the end of the drive, approximately two hundred feet (with my air horn). There was nothing on the road for some distance.

"Later in the day I went out to that area with my small dog. She refused to even walk and was trembling. This is the same dog that almost went through a screen door to attack the bear by our feeder a few weeks ago. I noticed an area of bent weeds that would have been where the creature had exited our woods, going into a small ditch, then back up to get onto the road before walking past our drive. On the road-side, in the direction I saw it going, there were three barefoot heel depressions, with faint toe marks, approximately twelve inches long. The area was very dry with fine gravel, so not a clear print.

"The week before, I had heard twigs snapping and weeds moving behind my fenced garden. This was approximately forty feet from the porch where I often sit. The dog barked. The noise stopped, then started again, so I fired off my air horn, which I always have near after an encounter with a large coywolf. The cabin sits around one hundred feet above the North Branch Lamoille River. There are many snowmobile and ATV trails, plus the long trail is only one-fifth of a mile.

It was very wooded and remote. A few homes and camps on our road."

Personal note: The property owner contacted me in late 2019 and sent me her story. I had visited her area in November of that year and noticed some animal activity in some of the wooded areas on her property. Her cabin neighbors the Lamoille River, and behind that is at least a mile of forested areas, giving it the ideal location for a hominid to seasonally migrate through the land undetected. Most of the eyewitness reports that I have observed, at least 80% of them, take place near a body of water. In many sightings reports I have read and personally investigated, it is fairly common for people to claim that Bigfoot sometimes completely disappears. Some claim that they are following tracks, and they suddenly stop, or they see the creature, start tracking it, and then it's gone.

VERMONT, JUNE 9, 2019

"I was up on Plymouth Road in Shrewsbury, Vermont, target practicing since it was so bright, warm and sunny out. While shooting, I kept hearing something in the brush behind me, at first, down near the marsh/swamp, then to my left or west afterwards ten minutes or so later. I never heard anyone or anything cross from the marsh across the road behind me to move in that direction into the thick woods, unless it happened while I was shooting with the earmuffs on.

"At the end of the road, the two roads make a T, to give you an idea of the area. With all the leaves on the trees and thick bushes, I couldn't see anything, but I kept hearing the brush moving around to my left or west. I was there maybe a half hour at most. I stopped shooting to collect all my brass casings on the ground and those left by others. This led me up the road to the gate. I proceeded up since there was more brass up there. That's when the wind shifted from the west;

that's when I smelled the odor of dead rotting fish! There is a swamp nearby, but I'm not sure there are enough fish to create that smell, and it came from the wrong direction; the swamp/marsh was to my south, not westerly.

"I felt as if I was being watched. The hairs on my neck stood on end, so that's when I decided to leave. Maybe it was Bigfoot, or maybe it was nothing, I'm not sure. But I wasn't sticking around to find out. I don't know of any animal I ever hunted that is not afraid of gunshots, so what in the world would move closer to a person shooting a .22 pistol? There were no others on that road I observed on my way out."

SUDBURY, OCTOBER 2019

"Hi there. I'm a seventy-two-year-old woman. I live in Sudbury, Vermont. My home is on a dirt road, and there is a swamp not too far away. We have a big Gauthier trash dumpster in our front yard that gets emptied once a month.

"Back in October 2019, at around 2:30 a.m., I was wakened by a loud crash. I thought something hit our house because I felt the floor shake. As I sat up, I saw my Doberman pinscher in the corner of the room shaking. (He never does that.) My husband was sound asleep, so I got out of bed and walked over to the window and looked outside, and I was shocked at what I was seeing. It looked like a large naked person covered in hair going through our trash. I could clearly see from the moonlight that our dumpster was tipped over, and this thing was picking through our garbage and making a mess in the yard. I tried to wake my husband, but he wouldn't budge.

"As I put my face up to the glass, I bumped my head on the window. That thing outside must have heard me because it stopped what it was doing and stood up, turned and looked directly at me. I could see its face and eyes glaring at me. This was not an animal. It looked so human, but it wasn't human. I'll never forget the eyes. Large, black, and menacing looking. I was frozen with fright. I couldn't move. After maybe a few seconds, it turned around and casually walked away towards the wooded area in back of our house, as if it was headed towards the swamp area. I'm not crazy, and I don't care what people think. I know what I saw."

Personal note: I met the husband and wife in November of 2019, and they gave me a tour of their home. I did notice how much forested land there was behind their home. Looking at a Google Earth map, the Sudbury Swamp was less than two miles from the house, so it would make for an ideal travel route for something to go unseen in the dead of night.

The time of year is also a key point. During the fall, mostly October and November, we see an uprise in eyewitness reports with these creatures going through trash, stealing garbage, raiding apple orchards, encounters with campers, etc. I'm drawn to the conclusion that here in New England when fall is upon us and vegetation dies out for the year, these creatures come out of their habitat and into ours in search for food.

And during the winter, they are following the deer migration as their primary source of food for the season. It has been surmised that the diet of Sasquatch is consistent with that of deer. It is believed they are omnivorous and opportunistic eaters like coyotes when weather isn't favorable. Berries and fruits are plentiful in the Bigfoot hot-spot regions. Bear is another plentiful and important food source that is believed to be a main protein source. Many sightings by hunters and hikers claim they saw a Sasquatch chasing deer, as well as witnessing them dragging or carrying a deer carcass on their shoulders. Digging up rocks and stacking them to find rodents has also been witnessed. Grasses, roots, larvae, carrion, elk, ducks, fish, and vegetables plucked from farms and gardens are also food sources of Sasquatch. Stories from early settlers in New England tell of Bigfoot stealing hogs and cattle from farmers. And because they don't have the claws or projecting canines of a carnivore, instead, they have manual dexterity and massive jaws with enormous, thickly enameled grinding teeth, allowing them to process foods unavailable to competitors like bears. Their size and presumed primate gut physiology could make it possible to digest and detoxify a wider range of plant materials, from lichens to alder leaves.

SEPTEMBER 15, 1972

"This is a story from my father, he said, when he was about fourteen or around this age. Now when he was younger, he was fast and won a lot of blue ribbons for track and field. So you know he was fast, and then one night he came face-to-face with his scariest nightmare, but before I do, let me tell you about where his sighting was. Well, Dad grew up in a farmhouse in Vermont. Essex County. His father used to raise pigs, cows and a few crops also. The nearest house was maybe three miles away; nobody would be in the woods trying to mess around with someone, no point.

"As I was saying, he grew up on his father's farm with his oldest sister and older brother and younger brother. One night he had to walk from somewhere, I forget where, but it wasn't a short walk in the park. You see, there were thick woods that he had to go through to make it home. This is the story told to me by my dad, he was walking home one night, and he was not scared of the woods, but he said it was about September 15, and it was starting to just turn dark, but the moonlight help him see. He said everything was fine when he smelled something awful. He said it smelled like a wet dog or something dead, maybe roadkill, but he said that it didn't spook him, and just thought nothing of it. He said to make it back home was about twenty minutes or so, but then the smell got worse and worse, and then he and it saw each other.

"He said it was just as shocked as he was when they saw the other one, and then he described the creature. He said it was very tall, as he stood on the top of a dried-up riverbed that he said had to have been eight to ten feet tall. And as he looked at it and it looked at him, they were looking directly in one another's eyes, but the thing was standing in the middle of the riverbed, so this thing was big with glowing red eyes, and he said it had long whitish hair.

"Needless to say, after that, he was running just like he saw a monster; then he said after that, he ran right into an old grave out in the middle of the woods. He said he hit his shins, and it hurt really bad. But he didn't stop for the pain because this thing could rip him apart limb from limb. It was so big, but he got home, and he said as soon as he got home, his older brother had a car, and he told him what just happened to him, but he didn't believe it, so my dad told him, 'Let's take Dad's rifle and drive to where I saw it.'

"They went to where he said he saw the thing, and then shining a light on the ground, he saw a giant footprint, and the footprint was about seven-foot strides in between steps. They didn't take any pictures of the footprints, but my uncle was a sheriff, and they told me they didn't have any reason to lie about this to me. I said, 'Why didn't you take any pictures?' They said it was just on the spur of the moment, and it was the early '70s; cameras were something you didn't just have on hand. That makes sense, but I wish they had, not for the world, just so the family could show real proof of the story."

VERMONT STATE LINE, 1975

"I spotted three (upright, bipedal, black/brown hair) on Route 4 heading into Whitehall in 1975 (four miles outside of town, heading west to east to Killington, VT) ... late fall, dusk, sleet/rain ... one crossed in front of me, coming out of the canal headed north, and when I slammed on my brakes, I saw two smaller ones cross behind me. The front one was big, seven feet plus; rear ones were maybe female and youngster, six feet and five feet but huge/broad. This was two years before the famous Whitehall sighting by the LEO that the movie was made of, not bear, and moved like Olympic athletes. No houses out there or any reason for any person to be out on that dark, lonely road.

"I'm an outdoorsman, backcountry survival expert, lived all over the country, know all game/predators; these were not mis-IDs. I was twenty years old with better than 20/20 vision, trained in observation. I'm still unsure what they are or why? Or why we have so little evidence (a body); perhaps a cover-up.

"I'm in PA now, mid-state, right on the Delaware River, and there are many sightings north of me near the Delaware Water Gap, perhaps seasonal, perhaps using the Appalachian Trail to migrate? I'm as perplexed today as I was after my '75 sighting.

"Half my maternal side family is from/settled the Bennington/West Dover, VT, area. Many stories up there from the old days. Forty-four years since I saw them, and now it seems like they're everywhere; back then I thought it was a northern Pacific coast phenomenon or Himalayan thing."

(WCAX) Channel 3
Published: Sep. 12, 2019

A Rutland County farmer is living a nightmare after discovering last Sunday that 13 of her meat goats were gone and seven were found dead. But just what killed the animals remains a mystery. A Vermont Fish and Wildlife biologist visited Falkenbury Farm in Benson Tuesday but was unsuccessful finding tracks from the predator. The farm's Jacki Ambrozaitis says seven of the goats were found dead Thursday but that six remain missing. The dead goats had bite marks on their heads and broken necks but otherwise were completely intact. Wildlife officials say if the goats were killed by a cat, they would have scratch marks, but there are no scratches. And because their bodies are intact, the hunter wasn't looking for food. Vermont Game Warden Lt. Justin Stedman says that makes domestic dogs the likely suspect. "It's like your house cat playing with a ball of yarn. To them, it's like they're playing, so they go out and things run, so they grab it and they shake it and it dies and then they go chase the next one," he said. But the warden isn't sure because some of the dead goats were large. Vermont Game Warden Spc. Robert Sterling says a dog or a wild coyote could be the killer. "We don't know for sure if it was domestic or wild, however the indications from the animals that I've seen leads towards it could be a wild coyote," he said. State wildlife officials granted the family permission to set traps out of trapping season to hopefully catch the predator. "They'll use a foothold style trap so if the animal turned out to not be a wild animal, that it wouldn't harm it, it would simply be able to be identified so they could find the animal that might be damaging the property and then it would safely be released," Sterling said.

As for the six missing goats, officials say they were either killed and eaten or ran off. "If anyone were to see some goats roaming around, definitely call the state police in New Haven, or call fish and wildlife, or if you know the farmer – they're from the area – to call them," Lt. Stedman said. Ambrozaitis says there is one neighbor with a dog who walks by, but it's always on a leash. Other neighbors know their dogs are not welcome on the farm. The 25 or so goats that survived are being kept in the barn. Ambrozaitis says she hates to see them cooped up, but since the attack was during the day, she's afraid to put them out in the pasture.

Personal note: I had visited the area several days after the incident, and although the locals were not very friendly to outsiders, they do keep a watchful eye out for trespassers and intruders. I found it interesting that 6 goats were reported missing with no signs of an animal predator. A failed attempt on the Vermont Fish and Wildlife's behalf to downplay the case as a dog or coyote as the guilty culprit. Any biologist would agree that this was NOT the work of a coyote or other K9 or large cat simply because of the sheer effort it would take to kill 7 goats and carry away an additional 6 overnight. Bite marks on their heads and broken necks indicate a predator with a high level on strength and cunning ability to carry out 7 kills overnight also tells me this was a joint venture effort with multiple predators.

TROY, MAY 2016

"I don't even know where to begin with this. To start, I'm a thirty-seven-year-old nurse from New Jersey. My husband and I and my nine-year-old daughter moved up to the town of Troy in 2010. We live in a mostly remote forested area, away from the trucks and city noise.

"After about a year, I started noticing things around the yard would come up missing. Sometimes tools from our shed would go missing for a few days, only to reappear in the backyard. During the summer, I noticed someone was stealing our vegetables from our garden. In just one night, all of our garden vegetables, which was ten by twenty yards, were gone. One time I saw our yard rake was on the roof of our house.

"Then in the spring of 2016, my daughter yelled to me from her bedroom. She said a 'strange gorilla man' was outside looking into her window. I never saw this 'person'; however, this was an ongoing thing for a while. She said it would come to her window and tap on the glass and growl at her. She was so terrified we put curtains over the window.

"Shortly after that, my two cats went missing. First my tabby cat, then my black cat three days later. I talked to coworkers about my issues, and one of them joked about Bigfoot. My husband has since installed outside motion-sensor lights with a home security system."

Personal note: The mother contacted me in 2017, and we talked over the phone a couple of times before I visited the property. Their home sits about 150 yards behind the main road, with plenty of shrubs and bushes in the front yard. The backyard has about four acres of land. The woods behind the house is heavily wooded and goes back at least a couple of miles. I did notice a small creek when viewing Google Maps. I suspect that was the direction of origin where it emerged from.

I examined the window from the outside, and measuring the height of the window, the suspect in question would've had to be at least eight feet tall for its head to reach the center of the window. When I interviewed the daughter, she described the creature as dark brown, having a pointy head, big black eyes, large square teeth, a flat nose with large nostrils, wide but thin lips, a square jaw, no facial hair but long hair in back. Once again, these creatures display a big interest in children, mostly females, and choose to interact with only one family member.

VERMONT

"I've lived in Vermont since I was seventeen years old. I'd never heard of Bigfoot nor seen anything like it in my life. I've seen black bears stand on their hind feet, take a few steps, but always returning to their four-legged walk.

"I married my husband in 1967 and had three children from 1970 to 1972. There are only two-lane roads in the state except for the interstate I-89, which goes from I-91 in Massachusetts into I-89 and winds its way clear to Canada. We lived in Windsor, Vermont, centered next to the Connecticut River nestled against Mount Ascutney. It's a truly beautiful place to live. The people are friendly even with their New England quirks. It's a place you'd bring up your children, let them walk to and from school, never had to lock your cars or houses, for everyone knew everybody for generations ... but one year changed my life forever.

"You see, my husband was a hunter. We drove to Richford, Vermont to his cousin's house, and he and his cousin would hunt buck or doe for the two weeks we stayed there. He knew every track an animal would leave and enjoyed the sport.

"So on that fateful afternoon coming back from Reading, Vermont, it was a typical day, maybe 80°, nice breeze. We were talking when I approached a long swinging corner. I had slowed a bit, but when I reached the straight, there was an animal in the center of the road. I came to a stop just yards from it. We both thought it was a bear, as it was hunched over with its back to us. I honked the horn a couple of times but to no avail; the creature continued doing its thing ... until it started standing up and up and up ...

"'It had to have been nine feet tall, maybe eight hundred pounds,' my husband said; reddish brown shaggy fur. Then it turned around. Neither of us could speak as it eyed us. It was very apparent that whatever it was, it was intelligent. It was a male but the largest animal I'd ever seen close up, and my husband was as shocked as I was at the sight of the thing (not being disrespectful). It eyed us for maybe a minute or two, looking directly into each of our eyes, then turned, took a step towards the side of the road, and one step it was on the grass, another step it was going into what the hunters called pucker brush because it had thorns two inches long or better, and it made you pucker for the pain it inflicted. Then the animal was just gone."

FINAL THOUGHTS

Over the decades, hair samples from Bigfoot have been recovered from many parts of North America. Many of these hairs have come back (not on file) with primate being the closest known animal. DNA is the best classification tool known to science, but there is not one centralized database that keeps DNA of Bigfoot. Many of my Bigfoot investigations have been very fragmented, mostly because of organizations being reluctant to share with others. Most researchers who have recovered hair samples understand that DNA is only recoverable in the follicle of the hair, and it deteriorates rapidly after being released from the species. One of the best methods to preserve a sample is to immediately put it in medical-grade alcohol and get it to a lab as soon as possible.

In chapter 7 of this book, it appears that these hominids on certain occasions make their own temporary dens. I have personally documented a few of them here in Vermont and New York. We know that certain animals in the wild go back to the location where they were born when they are ready to die. If a species such as Bigfoot is able to make it back to their place of birth, then perhaps we need to locate these places. The more difficult the trip into the caves and rough terrain may be, the more the likelihood of finding bones and other remains of these species.

The old newspaper articles that I have found are just a few of many of these stories of relic hominid bones found all over the United States in the 1800s to early 1900s during the construction of our modern-day road and railroad systems. Many of these stories have explained that mounds had been dug into, and giant-size human skeletons were found.

There are many hunters who have claimed to have shot a Bigfoot. They hear it scream after the shooting, but nobody has ever brought back or produced a body. The fact that these creatures are massive in size and superior in strength, I sincerely doubt that any rifle of any calibration will be sufficient enough to bring one down in a single shot. Therefore, I would strongly advise against trying to shoot one.

These creatures have a great ability to avoid detection and capture. They can also think and rationalize under pressure like most humans, and have the ability to adapt to changing conditions, environments and extreme weather conditions such as subzero temperatures.

During my research, I have found that these creatures share some human behavior such as traveling in family units. Some reports indicate two large adults seen with a smaller child or juvenile creature.

Audio recordings, also known as "the Sierra Sounds," show that they appear to have their own language that has not yet been deciphered. Despite their physical features that have a human quality, they also have communication styles, screams and other sounds that can be construed as human. There are numerous documented cases where the witnesses believe they hear two Bigfoot creatures communicating with some type of language. The conversational discourse has been described in different ways, but the part that remains consistent in each story is that one creature talks; the other one listens; then the other one responds in a very human interaction. For these hominids to have their own language shows a very high level of intelligence that many scientists choose not to acknowledge.

Lloyd Pye was doing research for years to prove that Bigfoot is part of a hominoid family and that humans are a genetic mutation. He believed this is a result of alien DNA being spliced together with Bigfoot DNA. Is it a possibility? Yes, there are some who think so. He claimed that these individuals are more suited for this planet than humans. Humans, on the other hand, are very fragile creatures. Our bones are thin, our eye sockets are small (which makes it hard for humans to see in the dark), and our walk is unbalanced on uneven terrain. According to Pye, there is not a single human bone in the so-called prehuman fossil record.

It is a well-known fact that big government has known about these creatures for decades but has kept it hidden from the public for reasons that go far beyond their justification of preserving the logging industry. Government generally sees citizens as stupid people who can't handle information or thinks we will do the worst possible things with information, so they hide it. This is true in every facet and level of government.

After examining the evidence for well over a decade, I have come to the conclusion that the Sasquatch is a species of unclassified subterranean human hybrids. However, although these hominids are clearly highly intelligent (perhaps second only to man) and elusive, I also know as a fact that the US and Canadian governments know that these creatures exist and are purposefully preventing discovery for both financial reasons and perhaps because of the potential dangers surrounding this species. But those dangers are not our safety, but for the possibility of a far-reaching discovery in their DNA.

ABOUT THE AUTHOR

Jason Lorefice, is a government contractor with a background in private investigation and is the author of Vermont Bigfoot Encounters and beyond. He has appeared on the Travel Channel along with various podcasts talking about the subject of Bigfoot. Jason spends his free time researching cryptozoology and the study of ancient giants that once roamed the earth.

Over the years, Jason has gathered a vast amount of evidence in the existence of these hairy hominids that have shared residence here in New York, Vermont, Massachusetts and all over New England for hundreds of years. Jason has also spent over 25 years in the field researching UFOs, alien abductions, mysterious cryptid monsters, ancient archaeological sites and other unexplained phenomena. Born and raised in Massachusetts, Jason currently resides in Williston, Vermont.

www.ingramcontent.com/pod-product-compliance
Lightning Source LLC
Chambersburg PA
CBHW032353280326
41935CB00008B/553